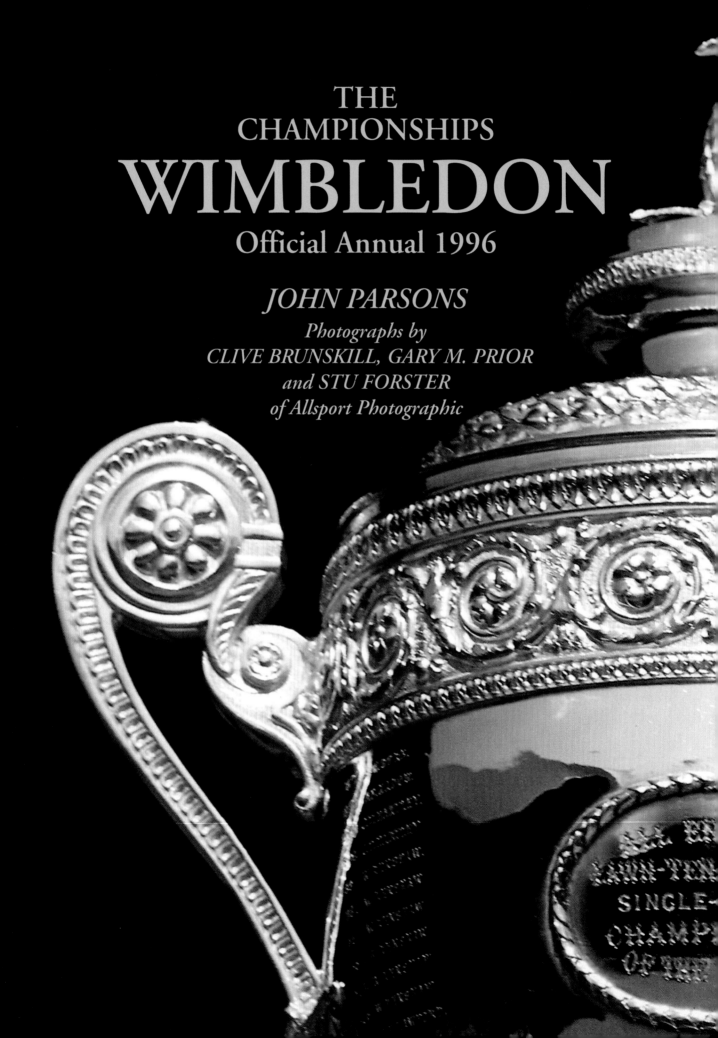

THE
CHAMPIONSHIPS
WIMBLEDON
Official Annual 1996

JOHN PARSONS

Photographs by
CLIVE BRUNSKILL, GARY M. PRIOR
and STU FORSTER
of Allsport Photographic

This first edition published in 1996 by Hazleton Publishing Ltd,
3 Richmond Hill, Richmond, Surrey TW10 6RE

ISBN: 1-874557-86-1

Printed in England by Ebenezer Baylis & Son Ltd, Worcester

Colour reproduction by Adroit Photo Litho Ltd, Birmingham

Results tables are reproduced by courtesy of
The All England Lawn Tennis Club

This book is produced with the assistance of Nikon (UK) Limited

Publisher
RICHARD POULTER

Production Manager
STEVEN PALMER

Business Development Manager
SIMON MAURICE

Art Editor
STEVE SMALL

Managing Editor
PETER LOVERING

Production Controller
CLARE KRISTENSEN

Photography
CLIVE BRUNSKILL
GARY M. PRIOR
STU FORSTER

Photo Research, Allsport
ANDREW REDINGTON
ELAINE LOBO

FOREWORD

The 1996 Championships were characterised by good sportsmanship. This behaviour continued through to the end of The Championships, which finished late on Monday evening with the final of the mixed doubles in front of an enthusiastic crowd who had enjoyed a wonderful day of tennis free of charge. Many spectators who had never before sat on the Centre Court thoroughly enjoyed the experience.

We had, as usual, many firsts during The Championships – the first Dutchman to win Wimbledon: Richard Krajicek – the first time anybody had won the men's doubles four times in a row in the modern era: Todd Woodbridge and Mark Woodforde – the youngest lady player to win a Championship event: Martina Hingis – the first singalong with Cliff Richard on a wet afternoon, and many other firsts.

After good weather in the first week, the second week tested the patience of the players, the fans, the staff and the media. In the end it was another great year with outstanding champions, particularly Richard Krajicek and Steffi Graf, winning for the seventh time, who both played superbly throughout the two weeks to achieve their Championship wins. The doubles winners also performed to a high standard, which we have come to expect.

However, what stands out for me was the behaviour and the fine character of the players. It was wonderful to see good sportsmanship and humility. Many players behaved in a way Kipling would have wished by treating those impostors 'triumph' and 'disaster' just the same. It is easy to behave well when you win. Many handled defeat with maturity, such as Todd Martin and Mal Washington to name but two.

As you would expect, we saw great skill, excitement, drama and fun, and I trust you will see all this reflected in this wonderful annual. It captures the essence of the 14 days of the 110th Championships.

I am sure you will enjoy the images reflected in the following pages.

John Curry (signature)

John Curry
Chairman
*The All England Lawn Tennis & Croquet Club
and the Committee of Management of The Championships*

ODUCTION

LONG before The Championships in 1996 began, everyone knew it would be a year of fond farewells. This after all was to be the final Wimbledon appearance by Stefan Edberg, who, in addition to achieving so much success at the tournament with his elegant skills since first making his mark as junior champion in 1983, had always been one of the game's finest ambassadors.

It would be his 14th bid for a title he had won twice, in 1988 and 1990, and although the prospect looked slight, the way he had played to reach the final of the Stella Artois tournament at Queen's Club two weeks earlier added sentimental support to the idea that 30 might not be too old for him to do so again.

Closer to home, Jeremy Bates, who first played at Wimbledon one year before Edberg, had also decided that at 34, despite reaching the last 16 twice in the four previous years, this would be his swansong.

Most significantly of all, however, Wimbledon was saying farewell this year to No. 1 Court, that delightful afterthought attached, like a limpet, to Centre Court two years after the present site for The Championships was developed in 1922. For all its apparent shortcomings and extensions, it remained the most intimate major tennis court in the world, which explains why some leading players, when learning that the arena would be replaced by a purpose-built big brother in 1997, reacted in terms akin to the 'You cannot be serious' phrase which John McEnroe introduced there in 1981 and which is now part of sporting legend.

No one needs added motivation when they compete at Wimbledon, especially the defending champions. Steffi Graf this time would be trying to add to the six titles she had already won, Sampras to make it what he called 'a four-Pete', after his third consecutive triumph 12 months earlier.

Both, when at their peak, had shown themselves to be the best grass-court players in the game but, going into Wimbledon '96, the odds on Sampras retaining his title were much longer than those on Graf, even though the German's preparations had been hit by a knee injury which meant she did not step on to a grass court for the first time in the year until 48 hours before The Championships began.

Sampras too was short of practice although in his case there were fears that the problem could be more serious for somehow his form earlier in the year, before injuries and then the tragic death of his coach Tim Gullikson in May, had lacked the conviction one had come to expect. Could therefore, the question was being asked, Boris Becker, boosted by his enthusiastic mood and form in winning at Queen's Club, win again after a break of seven years? Most of the bookmakers thought so.

As for Agassi, the 1992 champion and seeded three more on reputation than results, one could only guess how he might play after competing in only four matches in the previous three months but the general consensus, not least among his peers, was that he had not prepared well enough to give his basic talent the help it would still require.

How, one also wondered, would Yevgeny Kafelnikov, the Russian who had just won not just the French Open singles, for his first Grand Slam title, but also the doubles – a customary indication even on clay that someone can serve and volley far more than just adequately – fare? Tim Henman, Britain's best hope who had to face him in the first round, thought it offered him 'a great opportunity'.

Among the ladies, where Arantxa Sanchez Vicario again looked the most serious threat to Graf, there was to be the welcome return of Monica Seles for the first time since she was stabbed on court in Hamburg in April 1993. Seles had looked superb when winning the Australian Open, which Graf missed through injury, in January, but since then injuries and, more surprisingly, lack of self-confidence had set in. She had a favourable draw but would her damaged shoulder hold out? These and countless other intriguing issues would be resolved over the next two weeks.

MOST OF THE WORLD'S PR

THE TO

USE NIKON CAMERAS

THE T

VALUE YOUR PHOTO

pete SAMPRAS

1

USA Age: 24
World Ranking: 1

Motivation is never going to be a problem at Wimbledon for Sampras. He calls it 'the grand-daddy of all tournaments, the most important in the world'. And like Bjorn Borg, who set the modern record of five consecutive titles between 1976 and 1980, he says, 'It's a title you can never win too often.'

As champion in the three previous years, he was naturally favourite to maintain his success although there were also reservations – primarily his lack of match fitness during the first half of the year when injury and then the death of his coach Tim Gullikson meant, understandably, that there had been things other than tennis on his mind.

That explained why, after reaching the semi-finals of the French Open for the first time, he had nothing left to give emotionally or physically and flew home to recharge the batteries, hoping that 'when I walk through the gates of the All England Club those good feelings and memories will return and I'll come out ahead there again'.

boris BECKER

2

Germany Age: 28
World Ranking: 4

Winning the Australian Open in January, his first Grand Slam title for five years, had restored the German's appetite for major success and, although still second favourite to Sampras in the betting when The Championships began, the way he had won the Stella Artois Championships at Queen's Club two weeks earlier had greatly swelled his support. Becker, who will always be remembered for becoming the youngest and first unseeded champion when he was still only 17 in 1985, has always had the game to make him a principal contender for the most important title in the world.

Only once in the previous eight years had he fallen before the semi-finals and few would argue with his familiar theme that if he played well there was no reason why he could not beat everyone else on grass.

andre AGASSI

3

| USA   Age: 26 |
| World Ranking: 3 |

Although Wimbledon champion in 1992 and a semi-finalist a year earlier, Andre Agassi's prospects when he arrived for the 1996 Championships were very much an unknown quantity.

Since March he had played only four matches and won just one of them. At the French Open, where one would have expected to see his game coming together, he had looked overweight and undermotivated when losing to a fellow American, Chris Woodruff, who could hardly believe his luck at catching Agassi at such a time.

On the other hand, Wimbledon had lifted Agassi in the past and, as Sampras said, 'He's still got the best forehand, best backhand and best return of serve I've ever faced so you can never write him off.'

goran IVANISEVIC

4

| Croatia   Age: 25 |
| World Ranking: 7 |

Twice a finalist, Goran Ivanisevic began his campaign this year with mixed feelings. With a new coach, Vedran Martic, a fellow Croatian, he had begun the year magnificently, winning four of the first five tournaments in which he competed.

At the Lipton Championships in March, however, the big-serving left-hander woke up on the morning of the final with a neck injury, which meant he could hardly serve or hit backhands. Hard though he tried, his form and more especially his confidence had never been quite the same since.

'So much in my game has to do with confidence,' he says. 'Particularly in the Grand Slams, if I can get through the first two or three rounds which are often the toughest for me, it makes all the difference.

'If I know I am playing good, I know I can do it .'

yevgeny KAFELNIKOV

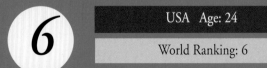

5	Russia Age: 22
	World Ranking: 5

Yevgeny Kafelnikov was the most popular choice as an outsider among the top eight seeds for the title. This was his third Wimbledon and from reaching the third round on his first visit he had improved to become a quarter-finalist in 1995, when he was beaten by Ivanisevic.

Hitherto there had been a question mark against the mental stamina of the thoughtful but sometimes over-emotional player from the Black Sea resort of Sochi, especially evident in the two previous Davis Cup finals.

Such doubts had been gloriously swept aside, though, just a month before Wimbledon when, at the French Open, he became the first player since John McEnroe at Wimbledon in 1984 to win both the singles and doubles at a Grand Slam. That and reaching the final of Halle on grass the weekend before Wimbledon proved that, in addition to being an all-court competitor, he could also succeed on all surfaces.

michael CHANG

6	USA Age: 24
	World Ranking: 6

At barely 5ft 8in tall, the American's prospects of winning Wimbledon are inevitably inhibited by his lack of height but, a quarter-finalist in 1994, he remains the type of player who can certainly do a good deal of damage to others rather than win the title for himself.

His restricted reach means that although he strikes some of the best passing shots in the game he can be dreadfully exposed on the rare occasions he goes to the net.

Chang had considerably improved his serve in recent years and his willingness to run until he drops, often retrieving what others would be content to let go, makes him an entertaining player to watch but the belief that he can succeed on grass still did not seem to be there.

thomas MUSTER

7

Austria   Age: 28
World Ranking: 2

This was to have been the first serious attempt by the Austrian left-hander to demonstrate that, at the highest level, he is much more than just a clay-court wonder.

In four previous visits Muster had lost in the first round and admitted that he had tended to fly in on the Sunday night without any grass-court preparation and totally without expectations.

Although unsuccessful when trying to retain the French Open title, Muster had proved himself a fast learner once he stepped on to grass courts by reaching the semi-finals at Queen's Club before losing to Stefan Edberg when the Swede was in top form.

Then in Halle, a few days before The Championships began, Muster aggravated the thigh muscle injury which put his belated Wimbledon ambitions on hold for another 12 months.

jim COURIER

8

USA   Age: 25
World Ranking: 8

A hardworking, textbook rather than instinctive player, Courier has struggled since 1993 to rediscover the form and the enthusiasm which kept him on top of the world rankings.

Few spank forehands with such ferocity and consistency as the American who usually favours wearing a white cap but there is a lack of surprise and subtlety in his game which can make life difficult for him on such a fast surface as grass.

Wimbledon runner-up in 1993, he was not expected to repeat that exciting progress this time, especially as he faced one of the toughest possible first-round challenges.

steffi GRAF

1	Germany Age: 27
	World Ranking: 1=

Such a strong favourite that even after being told on the eve of The Championships that she was suffering from a knee injury, former champion Martina Navratilova still said, 'I'd bet a lot of money on her winning again.'

The injury denied her a week of matchplay on grass at Eastbourne immediately before Wimbledon but that had not hindered her in the past when she had always chosen to practise rather than to compete in the two weeks after Roland Garros.

Her awesome forehand can be a match-winner on any surface, especially grass, but if that is going wrong she can sometimes look surprisingly vulnerable, even though her will-to-win still invariably rescues her in the end.

monica SELES

2	USA Age: 22
	World Ranking: 1=

Thrilled to be back for the first time in four years. She ran out of steam at the French Open and the extra pounds she had been carrying remained a potential problem if she was to become involved in many long matches.

Admits that although everyone, including former champion Martina Navratilova, has told her she has to come in more on grass, she still does not have the nerve to do so.

On the other hand her groundstrokes on both flanks are struck with such ferocity, accuracy and control that in most of her matches it does not matter. Had the boost of winning the first grass-court title of her career at Eastbourne 48 hours before The Championships began.

conchita MARTINEZ

3

Spain   Age: 24
World Ranking: 2

A new hairstyle this year but what was needed even more was a return to that fine competitive spirit and the easy flow of backhand passes which made her the champion in 1994.

Despite her ranking few would regard her as third in the list of most likely champions, not least because she does not impose herself firmly enough against opponents, even though she has the shots which could break down their defences.

Since winning the title two years earlier, she has failed to reach the final of any other Grand Slam event and took only four games from Graf on what should be her best surface, in the semi-finals of the French.

arantxa SANCHEZ VICARIO

4

Spain   Age: 24
World Ranking: 3

Although not a natural grass-court player, the Spaniard has a feisty approach and desire for success which means her prospects can never be discounted.

Over the years she has looked more and more confident at Wimbledon until in 1995 she reached the final and pressed Steffi Graf to 7–5 in the third in a classic encounter.

Her retrieving ability is second to none and although her moonballing, designed both to let her get her breath back and give her opponent something fresh to think about, can sometimes upset crowds, it is a legitimate tactic for which she will certainly never apologise. 'My job is to do what's best for me to win,' she says, reasonably.

anke HUBER

Germany   Age: 21
World Ranking: 5

5

Still encumbered by being regarded as 'the next Steffi Graf' whereas, despite her solid enough groundstrokes, including a forehand heavily dependent on top spin, she lacks the confidence and charisma of the champion from whose shadow she has been unable to emerge.

In six previous visits, the best she has managed is three appearances in the last 16. On her day she is certainly capable of justifying her seeding but, as with too many of the women players below the top handful, consistency of temperament, as well as in her game, is sometimes lacking. Too often the spectacular winners become forgotten as equally spectacular unforced errors undermine her effort.

jana NOVOTNA

Czech Republic   Age: 27
World Ranking: 6

6

In an age when stronger serving and intense drilling from the back of the court have become the dominant demand, Jana Novotna, as an all-rounder, has few peers. She can deliver, even within one game sometimes, a glorious range of winners, perfectly fashioned and delivered with exquisite timing.

The problem has too often been, however, that she finds it difficult to switch to percentage tennis in the moments of tension and on some of the big points, when that is needed.

She least of all has to be reminded of opportunities which have slipped away, including the Wimbledon title in 1993 when she looked poised to beat Steffi Graf in the final. But there is still time and she still has the game to win.

chanda
RUBIN

7

USA Age: 20
World Ranking: 7

Although Rubin, the daughter of a judge from Lafayette, Louisiana, had made her mark more on clay and hard courts since joining the Corel WTA Tour, there were many who felt that her best chance of really bursting through at the top would come on the grass at Wimbledon.

She had, after all, already demonstrated her ability to play well on the surface when her steadily improving serve, positive, flowing groundstrokes and confidence around the net had made her the junior champion four years earlier.

There was one huge snag – the wrist injury she suffered in April. It kept her out of the French and, although, determined to be fit for Wimbledon, she flew home after it flared up again at Eastbourne to consult the specialist who had been treating her, she reluctantly had to accept the medical advice not to play.

lindsay
DAVENPORT

8

USA Age: 20
World Ranking: 9

Two years earlier the Californian, who began playing tennis when she was seven, reached the quarter-finals at Wimbledon and with her height and strength was earmarked as someone with the qualities to begin pressing for the title in the not too distant future.

Few hit the ball harder off the ground and her enjoyment of doubles has also made her a confident volleyer. One problem remains, however: her lack of mobility, which too many of her opponents are only too ready to try and exploit.

Determined to try and fulfil her potential, she turned to Craig Kardon, former coach to Martina Navratilova, to see if he could help her in the same way but the partnership did not work out.

Increasingly these days, when the depth of competition in men's tennis is so considerable, even the most gifted top seeds can be vulnerable during the first one or two rounds of any Grand Slam. At Wimbledon, where the players, already nervous, also have to grapple with the unfamiliar bounce and sometimes perilously lush grass, the threat to hopes and reputations is all the greater.

So it was on the opening day of Wimbledon '96 when no fewer than four seeds – most notably third-seeded 1992 champion Andre Agassi – fell victim to opponents who, almost without exception, were quite simply better prepared on the day.

In the case of Agassi, overweight as well as under-prepared, one could be forgiven for thinking that he had stumbled again in a high-profile situation because he had lost the desire to compete, let alone put in the work beforehand which even the finest players need for their talent to be fully exploited.

A month earlier when he had lost to little-known fellow American Chris Woodruff in the second round of the French Open, the weaknesses were already obvious. And when, before a stunned No. 2 Court crowd, most of whom seemed to be teenagers who felt their world was falling apart with him, he lost to an even less well known American, Doug Flach, 2–6, 7–6, 6–4, 7–6, belief that too much money for playing too few matches had caught up with him with a vengeance was inescapable.

His abrupt elimination on the first day was the most unexpected early defeat of a champion or former champion while still supposedly a leading contender since the Australian, Peter Doohan, had upset Boris Becker, champion in the two previous years, in the second round of Wimbledon '87.

While few had expected Agassi to reach even the semi-final stages which his seeding suggested, no one, least of all Flach, was prepared for the humiliation awaiting the former world number one. It was more in trepidation than with

When Andre Agassi launched his Wimbledon bid, as shown on the previous pages, after needing help to push his way through an admiring throng to meet qualifier Doug Flach, no one thought he would be reinforcing No. 2 Court's reputation as the graveyard of the seeds.

Below: The Order of Play for Day One included some names 'out in the country' on Courts 7 and 15 that would be making news on rather bigger stages later in the fortnight.

The apprehension on Andre Agassi's face (below) was just as obvious as the unbelievable joy demonstrated by Doug Flach after a victory not only he will continue to talk about for years to come.

enthusiasm that Flach, better known beforehand as the brother of Ken, twice Wimbledon men's doubles champion with Robert Seguso, had accepted the invitation at the end of the qualifying rounds in Roehampton to pull out the names of the qualifiers to decide where they would be fitted into the draw.

'I bet if I do it, I'll be playing Agassi,' he said. He could never have dreamt

how lucky it would prove to be even though, despite the butterflies churning in his stomach when he first walked on to the court, he knew that he was match tight and that Agassi, quite apart from his other deficiences, clearly was not.

While Agassi arrived at Wimbledon having played only four matches since March, Flach had been plodding away, almost anonymously, in minor American satellite events, repairing a world ranking which had slipped into the 600s and was still only 281. Yet after a first set which Agassi breezed through comfortably enough, apparently playing well within himself, Flach started to unleash those big serves, including 22 aces, and wonderful passes which had helped him recover from two sets down against Anders Jarryd in the final round of qualifying – and the match took a dramatic turn.

Agassi, it was true, had spent several days after arriving in London recovering from a bout of influenza but the damage to his game had been done before then. His performance degenerated into a hapless mixture of errors laced with flurries of stupendous winners, though never enough of them. Too often he was slow and cumbersome, while his all-white outfit of baggy zip-up shirt and almost knee-length shorts hardly improved the athletic image.

When Agassi rallied from 0–3 in the third to have a point for 5–4, it looked as if he could pull himself round, just as he had after being down two sets to one against a qualifier at the Australian Open, but on game point he missed the easiest of forehands. Flach sensed another chance and took it, breaking for 5–4 and serving out to love, and although he perhaps wavered when missing his first match point, there was no lack of confidence or conviction in the forehand pass which earned him another at 7–6 in the fourth-set tie-break or the serve which Agassi then failed to return.

'I'm sorry for any disappointment I've caused to my fans,' said Agassi, who had hardly played with the heart of a champion. More than just letting down

Delight, too, for Jonathan Stark (left) after he powered his way to first-round success over a stoic eighth-seeded Jim Courier (below), while Michael Chang (bottom) was another seed to fall at the first hurdle.

his supporters, however, Agassi had let down himself.

The highest placed and least likely to fall of the other three seeds who were beaten was Michael Chang, who was eliminated by Alberto Costa. Although no one expected him to win the title, nor did anyone expect him to lose to a Spaniard who, although high enough ranked to have been seeded 16, had looked so ill at ease on grass when losing to Britain's Greg Rusedski in Nottingham a week earlier.

Chang and Agassi both lost on No. 2 Court, adding to the 'graveyard' reputation of this setting, although both knew that they and they alone were responsible for their early dismissals. Chang simply did not serve or return well enough against an opponent who also used drop shots well in a match which had little to offer *aficionados* of serve-and-volley tennis.

Perhaps it was the absence of his customary white cap which began the problems for Jim Courier when facing fellow American Jonathan Stark on Court Three. It soon became apparent, however, that the real threat was Stark's easy but potent ability to slam down heavy, full-length, variously directed serves which he then supported with brilliant volleys. Not only that but, apart from a brief spell when he rallied from 1–5 to 4–5 in the second set and provided himself with a lifeline by taking the third, Courier knew that his own second serves were likely to be rammed straight back past him, usually to his backhand corner. Stark won 6–2, 6–4, 2–6, 6–4.

Stark, coached by Brad Stein, who used to work with Courier, simply could not live with the power from an opponent who had first come to full notice in Britain a year earlier when, although they only met for the first time five minutes before their opening match, he partnered Martina Navratilova to success in the mixed doubles.

As for 15th-seeded Arnaud Boetsch, he must have thought he should be safe when he recovered from two sets down to force a fifth against 91st-ranked Ro-

manian-born German Alex Radulescu, who was to stay in the news, but despite leading 6–5 in the fifth, the Frenchman then double-faulted twice to lose the initiative and he went down 6–3, 6–4, 6–7, 5–7, 9–7.

Pete Sampras did not exactly have a straightforward start. Indeed when he was trailing by a set and a break against Richey Reneberg, a player more than capable of creating an upset on grass, he admitted he was 'starting to panic a bit', while others were checking record books

Pete Sampras had to work hard when he made the traditional Centre Court start by the defending champion and lost the first set before imposing his authority over fellow American Richey Reneberg.

Pictures tell the first day story. Jeremy Bates (right), in his Wimbledon farewell, felt the strain from the start against Nicolas Pereira but Chris Wilkinson (far right) provided British joy against Anders Jarryd.

Below: Stefan Edberg takes a breather between a host of winners which beat Guy Forget.

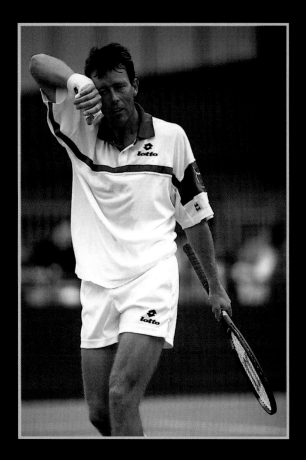

Opposite: Monica Seles adjusts the strings of her racket, which were tuned well enough on Day One.

in case they needed to mention that Manuel Santana in 1967 had been the last champion to lose in the first round.

In the end all was well for the title holder. Breaking back to 3–3 with a wonderful lunging forehand pass, he then settled down to serve, volley and, just as importantly, return with increasing confidence as he also overcame his initial foothold problems for a 4–6, 6–3, 6–3, 6–3 win. His only concern at the end was that Mark Philippoussis, the 6ft 4in Australian who had beaten him at the Australian Open, was also through to challenge him in the second round.

Of the favourites for the title, however, no one enjoyed Day One more than three-times former champion Boris Becker. He dismissed Frenchman Jean-Philippe Fleurian 6–0, 6–2, 6–3 in one hour 25 minutes and then had the triple bonus of seeing first Boetsch and Courier from his quarter and then Agassi, his projected semi-final opponent, being removed from his path.

Elsewhere Stefan Edberg, given the latest in a worldwide list of emotional welcomes in his retirement year, delighted the Centre Court crowd by beating Guy Forget 7–6, 5–7, 6–2, 6–2, while on the British front Chris Wilkinson, Colin Beecher and Claire Taylor flew the flag successfully on behalf of the wild cards. Beecher, playing for the first time, beat fellow British player Nick Gould 6–4, 6–4, 7–5 while Wilkinson took full advantage of changes in the draw following the withdrawal of Thomas Muster to reach the second round.

Wilkinson had originally been drawn to play Richard Krajicek, the Dutchman who had been moved to Muster's slot in the draw as the highest-ranked player not seeded and replaced by Jarryd, a lucky loser from the qualifying. The Southampton player, aiming to reach round three for a fourth consecutive year, again played above his normal tournament form to win 6–1, 6–3, 5–7, 6–2.

Taylor, who two years earlier had been warmly praised by Navratilova after giving the former champion a tough

start to her final year in singles, set up a second-round contest against Mary Pierce by beating Jo Ward 6–3, 6–2, while Samantha Smith, only just recovered from chicken-pox, played a resilient first set against 15th-seeded Irina Spirlea before losing 3–6, 6–1, 6–2.

Of the British men who fell at the first hurdle, the greatest disappointment, rather than surprise, was that Jeremy Bates, even though playing on Court 14, where he had enjoyed so many of his successes in previous years, lost to Nicolas Pereira, the sturdily built, heavy-hitting Venezuelan, who has never fully justified the potential he showed after winning the boys' singles title in 1988. Pereira, serving, driving and returning well, won 6–2, 6–3, 6–4.

Unlike the men, the leading women had their usual shock-free first day with Monica Seles and Conchita Martinez leading the way. Their turn to steal the headlines, though not in the way they would have wished, was still to come.

Germany's Bernd Karbacher had been looking forward to tackling fourth-seeded Goran Ivanisevic in the first round. After all, he had beaten the Croatian at the French Open and had been playing some of the best tennis of his life.

On the morning of the match, however, Karbacher, 27, slipped on the stairs at the house where he was staying and broke a bone in his right ankle. 'It was so swollen, I didn't really need a doctor to confirm the injury,' said referee Alan Mills, who then called up South African David Nainkin as a lucky loser. He did not last long. Ivanisevic won 6–2, 6–0, 6–2 in a mere 55 minutes.

The second day at Wimbledon is traditionally Ladies' Day, albeit in a more modest style than in years gone by when no men's matches were played and the main concourse became host to a fashion parade. In keeping with tradition, however, Steffi Graf duly opened play on the Centre Court and after a somewhat shaky few games against the 19-year-old Czech Republic player, Ludmila Richterova, who possesses an imposing serve, as well as a statuesque appearance fit for a model, the defending champion lifted the tempo for a comfortable 6–4, 6–1 win.

In truth, though, this was Britain's Day. By the end of one of the greatest afternoons for British tennis which most people could remember, Greg Rusedski, Mark Petchey, Danny Sapsford, Luke Milligan and, above all, Tim Henman had joined Colin Beecher and Chris Wilkinson, who had earned second-round places the day before.

Not since 1976 and only twice before since Open tennis began in 1968 had Britain had seven players through to the second round, which was cause in itself for joyous celebration. What made it all the more fantastic, however, was that the last of those seven victories was a 7–6, 6–3, 6–7, 4–6, 7–5 victory for Henman over the Russian, Yevgeny Kafelnikov, who just over two weeks earlier had won not just the singles but also the doubles at the French Open.

In a remarkable match lasting three hours 36 minutes, Henman, who had climbed from a world ranking of 240 at the 1995 Wimbledon to 62 this time, really came of age in deservedly beating one of his junior contemporaries, who had spurted well ahead of him to be fifth in the world list – and the seedings.

The result was marvellous enough but the manner in which it was achieved was even more so. It was Henman's first match on the Centre Court and also the first singles he had played which had spanned the full five sets. It had become an astonishing emotional roller-coaster as Henman, apparently in line for a

straight-sets success at one stage, let Kafelnikov escape to win the third set from 0–40 at 3–3 and then to hold the fourth from 0–40 and 3–4.

Not content with that, Henman, still seeking his first win over an opponent in the top ten, was also broken in the opening game of the fifth and at 3–5, 15–40 faced two match points. The remaining 16 minutes of an epic encounter, however, were great theatre. Henman, who in the past had been accused of not having a match-winning shot and not a reliable enough serve to make him a world-class player, not only saved the first match point with an ace but also the second.

Suddenly the crowd began to fuel the drama. All along there had been a buzz of expectation but also a feeling that perhaps they should not get too excited lest the enthusiasm fade into disappointment, as when Andrew Castle lost a two-sets-to-one lead against Mats Wilander and Chris Bailey was denied victory over Goran Ivanisevic by a second-serve ace.

Over those last few games they were mentally hitting every serve, pounding every drive, calling every line and suffering the anguish of near-misses with Henman, especially when he broke back to 5–5, helped by another crucial Kafelnikov double fault, and then saved another break point in holding for 6–5.

The tension for the spectators was almost unbearable as what proved to be the final game unfolded. Yet Henman, three months short of his 22nd birthday, and 364 days after he had become the first player to be disqualified at Wimbledon for hitting a ball in anger which then accidentally struck a ballgirl, remained outwardly cool and steadfast, masking the cramps which were beginning to creep in. The 16-stroke rally which eventually carried Henman to match point was a classic, including a stupendous retrieving lob from the Russian which effectively brought it back to square one, but then after a couple more exchanges the

Tim Henman's forehand winners had the Union flags waving on Centre Court as he achieved the finest British victory in the men's singles for a decade by beating fifth-seeded Yevgeny Kafelnikov (below). The Russian served well enough but simply could not resist the quality or consistency of Henman's returns.

Ladies' Day was turned into British Men's Day. Right: Greg Rusedski salutes the crowd for their cheers after he beat Canadian Daniel Nestor on No. 1 Court. Below: Mark Petchey concentrating well on his volleying against Leander Paes.

Danny Sapsford (above) had been Britain's first winner of the day, supported even more spectacularly by Luke Milligan, who twice recovered from being a set down to upset Sweden's vastly more experienced Jonas Bjorkman.

Below: Clare Wood, the British number one, lifted domestic spirits by taking the first set but was just unable to sustain the effort against Germany's Claudia Porwik.

Below right: Brenda Schultz-McCarthy prepares to launch another of her powerful deliveries while beating South African Joanette Kruger.

British number one hit a scorching cross-court forehand.

It was 6.46 p.m. on the Centre Court clock. Kafelnikov's first serve was a fault. The second was right and again a rally started to develop with the Russian convinced that Henman's second return was long. But it was not. It caught the back of the line. Three shots later Kafelnikov's backhand landed in the net and British tennis was celebrating the most spectacular domestic victory since John Lloyd had knocked out fourth-seeded Roscoe Tanner in 1977.

The grandson of Henry Billington, the former British Davis Cup and Wimbledon player, and great grandson of Ellen Stawell-Brown, who was the first lady to serve overarm at The

Championships, was exultant but remained as calm as he had been throughout the match. With a masterly touch of understatement, he described the delivery of two aces to save match points at 3–5, 15–40 in the final set as 'timely'.

'When I missed those opportunities at 0–40 in the third and 0–40 in the fourth, the pressure was on because I was getting pretty close to the finishing line. Yes, self-doubts creep in but then you feel I've got nothing to lose. Let's go for it and once I broke back to 5–5 it was a huge boost to my confidence and my energy levels.'

While Henman was the last British winner of the day, Danny Sapsford, his next opponent, had been the first. De-

spite trailing 0–4 in the opening set against Australian qualifier Peter Tramacchi, the 27-year-old from Weybridge, who had retired for nine months in 1992 while seeking enough sponsorship to return to the tour, hit back on Court Three for a 7–5, 6–4, 6–3 victory.

Sapsford, ranked 195, had never previously won a match at Wimbledon in the main event, the qualifying or the juniors. 'It was a case of 11th time lucky,' he said. 'I feel as if I've exorcised a demon.'

Luke Milligan's 4–6, 6–1, 2–6, 7–5, 6–4 defeat of Sweden's 64th-ranked Jonas Bjorkman was even more astonishing. It was the 19-year-old Muswell Hill player's first win in other than satellite events and the first time he had played in a Grand Slam match.

'It was all a matter of confidence,' said the slim right-hander ranked 278 in the world. 'Once the first set was over the novelty of being here wore off and I played a very good second set,' said Milligan. Even so it was his ability to recover again after losing the third against a vastly more experienced opponent who had been a semi-finalist on grass in Rosmalen ten days earlier which was so impressive, not least the way he ended the match with his 14th ace.

Mark Petchey's 1–6, 6–2, 6–4, 7–6 victory over Leander Paes on Court Two was also a notable victory. Ironically, while Petchey's Davis Cup record is one he would rather not reflect upon, the Indian plays by far his best tennis in that competition and beat the Essex player in a World Group qualifying round tie in New Delhi in 1992. In a thrilling climax to a match packed with a contrasting galaxy of stylish and powered winners, Petchey eventually won on his fourth match point in a 13–11 fourth-set tie-break, after having his first at 5–4 in the set.

While Henman was tantalisingly close to his joyous success, the screaming cheers echoing from Court No. 1 let everyone know that Greg Rusedski, despite needing three days of intensive therapy and acupuncture to treat a dis-

placed hip, had beaten Daniel Nestor, one of the Canadians he had left behind when he became a British player just over a year earlier.

The match, as expected, was dominated by huge serving. Rusedski struck 30 aces and the match was well into the third set before there was even the first break point. It went to and was won by Rusedski. The grin was wider than ever.

Britain's only success in the women's singles came from Lancashire's Florida-based Rachel Viollet, whose 6–2, 2–6, 6–1 victory over another Florida-based Brit, Megan Miller, also made her the highest-ranked British player in the world rankings, although only because Clare Wood had lost to Germany's Claudia Porwik 2–6, 7–5, 6–4 after failing to make a return in court on three match points at 5–4 in the second set.

As for those expected to be still chasing honours in the women's singles late in the second week, there were few problems, least of all for Mary Joe Fernandez, who trounced Jana Kandarr 6–0, 6–0, while it was plain sailing too for Arantxa Sanchez Vicario, Jana Novotna and Martina Hingis on a day when the one name on most people's lips was Tim Henman.

There was hardly any need for Arantxa Sanchez Vicario to look over her shoulder in her first-round match. The 1995 runner-up was not at her best but still won 6–3, 6–4 against Italy's Adriana Serra-Zanetti.

day 3

Monica Seles never found the groove she needed to stay in control against Slovakia's Katarina Studenikova before a stunned No. 1 Court crowd.

At the outset, Day Three promised to be relatively straightforward after the excitement of the first two. There were hopes, of course, for more British success but nothing which, on paper at least, should cause further embarrassment to those with genuine chances of taking home the titles.

How wrong that was. Just after 7 p.m. and following a minor delay for drizzle when she had been leading 3–2 in the final set, Monica Seles, joint number one in the world and Wimbledon's second seed, was beaten 7–5, 5–7, 6–4 by Katarina Studenikova, a slim 23-year-old from Bratislava she had beaten 6–1, 6–1 on her way to winning the Australian Open in January.

For the crowd on Court No. 1, most of them originally more concerned about the Tim Henman–Danny Sapsford contest due to follow, it was a stunning upset. And yet the warning signs had been there when a similar lack of self-belief and conviction led to Seles's losing to Jana Novotna at the French Open three weeks earlier.

Hard-court tactics had served Seles well enough when she won the Direct Line Championships at Eastbourne on her way into Wimbledon but even then there was always the risk that her reluctance to go to the net, other than in the first few games when she was telling herself what she *had* to do or later when forced to do so, might prove her downfall.

That, coupled with her lack of match practice because of the shoulder injury which kept her competitively inactive from early February to late May and the extra pounds she was carrying, added to the concern of those around her, hoping beyond hope that her normal iron will would carry her through to the only Grand Slam title which still eludes her. Instead, three days into Wimbledon '96, she was gone, suffering her earliest defeat in the 18 Grand Slams she had played since her first in 1989.

Seles, who began sliding into serious trouble when she lost five consecutive games from 5–3 in the first set, said, 'I'm not too happy with the way I'm playing at the moment but I'm determined to learn from my mistakes. When I beat her in Australia, she made lots of errors. This time I made them. I had my opportunities but simply didn't take them.'

That was certainly the case when, following a fairly short rain delay which

Studenikova welcomed more than the naturalised American, because she was starting to wane from the mental, rather than physical pressure, Seles moved from 3–2 to 4–2 but missed a point for 5–2 and did not win another game in the match.

'She went for her shots and attacked. I didn't,' said Seles, puffy-eyed and looking a little bewildered. 'I know I have to go for my shots fearlessly like I did last week and not be timid. But there's a lack of confidence right now which I have to get over.'

One could tell, once the grunting level began to move to a peak early in the second set, that Seles was in trouble. It was evident that, however much other players might be intimidated by the thought of the pummelling shots they expected to be facing from the other side of the net, Studenikova, a modest 59th in the world rankings, was not. 'Since Australia I knew I'd improved my serve and been playing far more aggressively so I felt that on grass, which we know she doesn't like, I'd have a good chance of beating her.'

Studenikova says that Steffi Graf is her favourite player and there were times when it was possible to imagine it was the German, not a Slovakian, who was pulling Seles so easily from side to side and then passing an increasingly breathless opponent. As well as being another pony-tailed, tall blonde, Studenikova employed the same exaggerated slice on her backhand which kept the ball low and then gave her the opportunity to run around the returns and hit cross-court winners, often into open space, on the forehand. Zina Garrison had played much the same way to beat Seles, also on Court No. 1, in 1990.

The Seles defeat was the major tremor but there were other upsets in the ladies' singles as both the 14th and 15th seeds, Amanda Coetzer and Irina Spirlea respectively, were also knocked out. Coetzer, from South Africa, whose lack of height is always going to be a problem for her on grass, was beaten none too

surprisingly 7–6, 2–6, 6–3 by the American, Meredith McGrath, an accomplished grass-court player. Then Spirlea, who had already been given a fright by Britain's Sam Smith, lost 6–3, 2–6, 6–4 to Argentina's Ines Gorrochategui.

Elsewhere among the ladies, Arantxa Sanchez Vicario and Anke Huber continued to make progress, the latter with almost embarrassing ease, 6–2, 6–1 against Pam Shriver, who would certainly have preferred to make her expected farewell as a player at Wimbledon other than by a serve on match point

Varying the pace and angles of her returns, Studenikova kept up a pressure which Seles, struggling with her serve as well as her mobility, could not resist.

Overleaf: Pam Shriver relished every moment of what was likely to be her final year in singles at The Championships.

which bounced in her own service court and only then over the net.

It was not until 7.10 p.m. that the perplexed Seles and overjoyed Studenikova vacated Court No. 1 to make way for Henman and Sapsford. Henman was immediately into his stride, racing through the first set 6–1, but Sapsford grabbed the initiative in the second as the court surface dampened and the light faded until the Oxfordshire player broke back to 4–5 and held for 5–5, at which point, at 8.37 p.m., they were sent home overnight.

That meant Luke Milligan, the 19-year-old son of a London taxi driver from Muswell Hill, had to wait to see which one of them would be his next challenger after he had continued his encouraging breakthrough in the bravest and most dramatic fashion. It was not until his eighth match point, one hour 50 minutes after his first, that the slim, dark-haired right-hander beat Nicolas Lapentti from Ecuador, a former world number one junior, 6–4, 6–2, 6–7, 6–7, 6–1. The match lasted three hours 46 minutes, on top of the two hours 51 minutes he had played in the first five-setter of his life the day before, so it was hardly surprising when, as the first match-winning chances began to slip away at the end of the third set, Milligan started being troubled by cramp.

It seemed to come to a peak immediately after he had broken and was ready to serve a second time for the match at 6–5 in the fourth set, when he collapsed on the court. Because several of their tournaments are played in conditions of extreme heat, the ATP Tour allows treatment of players suffering from cramp or other forms of dehydration but elsewhere, including Wimbledon, cramp is a 'loss of conditioning' rather than an injury and therefore treatment is not allowed.

'In that fourth-set tie-break the cramp hit me badly in both legs,' said Milligan. 'I was really struggling. It was a matter of trying to put one foot in front of the other.' Milligan lost the tie-break 7–3 and was hardly heartened by his be-lief that Lapentti, ranked almost 200 places above him, was looking fresh. Fortunately for Milligan that was not so. Suddenly his opponent also began grabbing his leg in agony. 'When I saw he was cramping as well, that gave me a boost,' he added.

Lapentti's resilient serving denied Milligan his first five match points which began at 6–5 in the third set and continued at 5–3 in the fourth and 5–0 in the fifth. In all the circumstances it took enormous courage by Milligan to sustain his determination, especially after he double-faulted on the sixth match point at 5–1 in the final set and netted a forehand on the seventh.

Finally, though, Milligan, whose serve and forehand, always his strongest points, had both become potential match-winning weapons, created match point number eight with another of those flashing forehands which brought gasps of approval from the crowd on Court No. 13 and then he went up to put away a backhand volley off the return of a second serve.

It was a win which not only guaranteed Britain a place in the fourth round but made sure he would be banking at least £15,900, more than he had been used to winning in a whole year. 'It'll certainly take a hell of a lot of [financial] pressure off my parents,' he said.

Colin Beecher's hopes of reaching the third round ended when, despite trying to serve and volley his way to success against Italy's Renzo Furlan, he was never quite able to do so well enough, long enough to prevent falling prey to his opponent's superior passing skills when it most mattered.

Thomas Enqvist, the ninth seed, became the latest victim in the men's singles, losing 6–4, 7–6, 6–3 to the 20th-ranked American, MaliVai Washington, but in terms of grass-court abilities that was anything but surprising and almost forgotten, except by Washington, of course, who could already see the draw opening up for him, amid the calamity for Monica Seles.

A triumphant wave from Luke Milligan as he leaves Court 13 after beating Nicolas Lapentti.

Below: Colin Beecher battled hard but it was not enough against the more experienced Italian, Renzo Furlan, on No. 3 Court.

Doug Flach successfully followed up his remarkable first-round defeat of Andre Agassi by beating another American, Jared Palmer, 2–6, 6–3, 6–3, 6–4 but then found he had problems off the court. The 1,000–1 shot had forgotten to extend the booking of his hotel room in the excitement of beating the former Wimbledon champion. 'Two days in a row now I've received messages from them asking, "When are you leaving?" Hopefully they won't kick me out just yet.'

'To change the surface here
would be the biggest mistake
for tennis. Even though most
of the points may be quick,
getting rid of the grass would
be wrong. It would also be
the biggest mistake this club
could ever make. It still has
so much tradition. It is
history.'

*Pete Sampras when asked if it was time for
Wimbledon to dig up the grass.*

WIMBLEDON

day **4**

THURSDAY 27 JUNE

The packed crowd on No. 1 Court provided Stefan Edberg with a prolonged standing ovation as his memorable 14-year Wimbledon career came to an end.

chasing what would have been his 50th singles success at the tournament and the 100th match win of his career on grass, Stefan Edberg found himself edged out 4–6, 6–4, 7–6, 6–4 by a fellow Swede playing in the event for the first time, Mikael Tillstrom.

'It'll seem strange walking off knowing it was for the last time,' said Edberg, 30, who at the end of the match, after his opponent had sensitively left him to accept the full tribute alone from a still packed Court No. 1 at 8.54 p.m., sat for some time on his courtside chair, savouring the moment.

'It had to end at some time and today was the day,' said Edberg, whose only disappointment was that he had not served so well as he would have liked in a match he clearly felt beforehand he could win. 'I'd rather have finished on Centre Court but I wasn't crying out there at the end. It's been so great to be here and once you've been a champion here you like to leave like one. The great thing is that as a singles champion, you're always a member here – and always welcome to come back.'

The immaculate skills were still there as Edberg fought to the last, urged on, frantically at times, by spectators, three of whom were rewarded when they caught the three sweaters he threw among them at the end.

Although Sampras had looked shaky enough in the first round against Richey Reneberg on Monday to prompt fears that he might again be vulnerable under the weight of the Philippoussis serving, the concern lasted only until the American had grabbed an initiative he was never to lose by winning the tie-break at the end of the first set.

'The difference this time was the surface, grass not Rebound Ace, and the fact that the way he played in Australia was phenomenal,' said Sampras after his highly proficient 7–6, 6–4, 6–4 victory. 'I just won the bigger points today,' added the American, typically underplaying the added all-round skill which brought that about.

On the day defending champion Pete Sampras demonstrated how determined he was to win for a fourth time by handing a salutory lesson to Mark Philippoussis, the swashbuckling server who had trounced him at the Australian Open, one of the game's most respected elder statesmen among champions was bowing out of The Championships.

Playing his 14th Wimbledon and

In a match which for the first two sets at least was all about who could best return the other's serve, Philippoussis flung down one serve of 131 mph and several second serves of between 126 and 128 mph but some of his work in support was not so potent, such as the volley he missed to give Sampras his chance at 6–4 in the crucial tie-break. Thereafter, although Philippoussis continued to go for the big shots, Sampras was varying pace, angles and tactics in general. The low backhand dipping volley which earned him break points in the first game of the second set after the teenager's volley was once again not firm enough was a joy to behold, as were the two passes which gave Sampras the break for 2–1 in the third.

Perhaps it was not quite the lesson for Philippoussis which some suggested but Sampras certainly offered the 6ft 4in Australian some sensible advice when he said, 'He's got a huge game but he just needs to tone it down a little and maybe not hit every second serve as hard as his first.' Philippoussis hit 28 aces, 20 of them by the seventh game of the second set, but, as he observed, 'I'd prefer to serve no aces and win than serve 500 aces and lose. My first volleys are more important than smacking away on my serve but I'm still young. I'm sure I'll learn that as I get on.'

Unlike the bottom half of the draw where only three seeds out of eight made it to the last 32, the six at the top of the

Pete Sampras (below) avenged his defeat at the Australian Open in his big-serving battle against Mark Philippoussis.

top half all went through, with Michael Stich winning another late-night encounter against Shuzo Matsuoka. Cedric Pioline outclassed Britain's Mark Petchey 6–1, 6–4, 6–2 with near-perfect serving and returning while Goran Ivanisevic dropped only 15 points in 16 service games in a 7–5, 6–4, 6–4 win against Pierre Bouteyre, a qualifier from France whom not even most French journalists knew much about. They could be forgiven. Bouteyre, 24, built like a strong-running rugby player, arrived to qualify for Wimbledon with a world ranking of 496 without ever having played either a Tour or Grand Slam event before and had never stepped on to a grass court. Indeed he only decided to 'give it a try' because his ranking had been too low for him to have been accepted into the qualifying for the French Open a month earlier.

On the British front there was more disappointment than delight but not really surprise, merely a return to the old familiarity as domestic players were beaten by higher-ranked opponents. Yet it need not have been that way. Chris Wilkinson's 1–6, 7–5, 5–7, 6–4, 6–3 defeat by Jan Kroslak of Slovakia was the most frustrating because he had been a break up in both the second and fourth sets and in the latter had two points for a double-break 3–0 lead.

It was much the same story of missed opportunities as Greg Rusedski, ranked 65th in the world, slipped to a 7–6, 4–6, 7–6, 6–2 defeat against the New Zealander, Brett Steven, six places above him. 'I certainly had my chances in the first set,' said Rusedski, who rallied from being a break down to have a point to go ahead in the first-set tie-break, only to net a forehand when there was a clear chance for a winning pass.

Steven, a solid, all-round performer, eventually won that tie-break 9–7 but only after Rusedski not surprisingly looked hard and long at the line after a return which seemed to have just clipped the edge was called out on the set point. There were three more set points for Rusedski in the 14–12 third-set tie-break

which effectively settled the outcome for, from then on, Steven was in control.

Rusedski hit 30 aces but, even so, his defeat meant that, since reaching the last 16 at Wimbledon amid much euphoria in his first matches as a British player in 1995, he had gone a full year without advancing beyond the second round of a Grand Slam.

Three qualifiers were still making ecstatic progress. Apart from Doug Flach and Neville Godwin, already through, Mose Navarra turned No. 3 Court into Little Italy for a while during the afternoon when, in his first tournament on grass and his first five-setter, he upset 17th-ranked Spaniard Alberto Costa 4–6, 7–6, 3–6, 7–5, 9–7. The roar of celebration when the sturdy Italian raced the full width of the court to hit a screaming forehand winner down the line to level the match at two sets all could be heard all the way out at No. 13 Court.

In the ladies' singles, Britain's interest ended when Rachel Viollet and Claire Taylor, both ranked below 200, were not unexpectedly sent packing by opponents of much higher stock. On a day when

During the first week, a famous Lord of the Manor title, the lordship of Wimbledon, fetched a world record price of £188,000 when it was sold at auction by the Princess of Wales's brother, Earl Spencer.

Boris Becker, who had declared an interest in purchasing the title, denied that he was the buyer and now a lord. 'I am quite happy with just being Boris Becker,' he said.

In another big-serving battle, New Zealander Brett Steven (left) hit more winners than Britain's Greg Rusedski.

Below: HRH The Duke of Kent, President of the All England Club, watched the day's matches on Centre Court intently.

Monica Seles was not the only early victim among the seeded lady players. Lindsay Davenport (below) was outshone in most aspects of the game by Larisa Neiland.

for no particular reason no fewer than three British newspapers likened events surrounding – or action by – three different British players to Noël Coward, Viollet lasted only 40 minutes when she went out in the midday sun against Martina Hingis. The Swiss miss was then still only 15 and already seeded 16. 'She has so many shots to choose from,' said the American-based Viollet, wistfully.

Second on Court Four, where Wilkinson had lost earlier, was Claire Taylor, the Oxfordshire girl coached by her namesake, the unrelated Roger Taylor. She was playing Mary Pierce, the American-based French import from Canada whose apparently haughty gestures do not appeal to everyone. She arrived eight minutes late – a tactical ploy perhaps? – and continued in somewhat aloof vein, trying to shrug off the scrum of photographers squeezed into the side of the court, as well as the errors she was forced into making by a determined but not quite experienced enough opponent. Pierce took seven of the last eleven games as Taylor ran out of ideas to win 6–4, 6–2.

Two more seeds were knocked out, both curiously enough on No. 2 Court, leaving ten of the original starters to move into the third round. Lindsay Davenport, seeded eight, succumbed with dismal ease to Latvia's reliable Larisa Neiland 6–3, 6–2. Then Magdalena Maleeva, seeded ten, lost a titanic struggle against Nathalie Tauziat, a French player who had proved her grass-court qualities by winning at Eastbourne 12 months earlier.

Tauziat saved four set points in the opening-set tie-break which went to 9–7 and then in the final set recovered from being a break down, the second time when Maleeva was serving for the match, before taking it on her fourth match point.

At the other end of the seeding scale, defending champion Steffi Graf made heavy weather of beating the lowly ranked 23-year-old Italian, Nathalie Baudone, who had won only three matches earlier in the year. Graf stepped up her form in the second set but seemed to be troubled again by her injured knee. 'It wasn't great today,' she said, referring to the knee, but it could just as well have been about her tennis. Conchita Martinez, the 1994 champion, beat Lisa Raymond in a none too spectacular match on the Centre Court, 7–5, 7–5.

Martina Hingis, seen here beating Britain's Rachel Viollet, won a growing number of admirers, even before the excitement of her doubles triumph, with her happy, as well as stylish, approach to her tennis.

WIMBLEDON

day 5

FRIDAY 28 JUNE

It never rains but it pours, they say. That was certainly true on Day Five of Wimbledon '96. Not only did the rain first delay and then disrupt play for longer than during the whole of the three previous years when just a total of three hours was lost but another of the game's most charismatic figures was eliminated.

The first-round defeat of Andre Agassi and second-round departure of Monica Seles had been disappointing enough but at least they only had themselves to blame for what happened. In the case of Boris Becker, his failure to get through his third-round match against 223-ranked South African qualifier Neville Godwin was the outcome of a fluke injury.

Although Becker had not been playing at his best, making a surprising number of unforced errors during a set in which he twice broke to take the lead but then immediately surrendered the advantage, no one was prepared for what happened in the 58th minute of the match during the initial point of the first-set tie-break.

Godwin hit a second serve which Becker struck with the frame – but very late. Instantly the racket dropped from his hand because of the pain he was already feeling in the lower part of his arm and the second seed knew straight away that the injury was serious. Although after treatment he went through a few practice service swings and tried flexing his wrist, he told umpire Richard Kaufman, 'I can't hold my racket,' as he beckoned Godwin to the net where he told him, 'Sorry I can't carry on.' His only consolation was that the problem turned out to be a severely sprained tendon rather than the broken bone or severed tendon he had initially feared.

Becker said that as he was making the return he 'felt something pop'. The look of dismay on his face told its own story. The German, who had been out of action for two months after winning the Australian Open with a virus and then missed the French Open because of a thigh injury, said: 'I guess this injury feels much worse because I was one of the few who had a serious chance of winning the whole thing this year. I was playing great tennis. The draw didn't look too bad. It's a serious disappointment. After winning at Queen's Club I felt I was ready for something major here.

'If there's one tournament in the year when I most want to do well it's Wimbledon. Injuries never come at the right time. I've been injured before and I know it's just part of the deal when you're an athlete. At the end it evens itself out but over the last few months I've been on the wrong side of it. You have periods when you have plenty of luck and then you have periods when the luck isn't on your side and you seem to run from injury to injury. But coming at Wimbledon is as bad as it can be.'

This was not the first time that his interest in The Championships had ended with him being taken to hospital for X-rays. Becker's first Wimbledon as a 16-year-old in 1984 came to an abrupt halt when he fell while playing the American, Bill Scanlon, on Court Two and had to be taken off in a wheelchair with a broken ankle. Twelve months later, of course, he returned to become the youngest and first unseeded men's singles champion.

Becker's elimination reduced the number of seeds in the bottom half of the draw from the original total of eight to just two – Wayne Ferreira and Todd Martin, both of whom still had second-round business to keep them occupied. If ever there was a time when one half of the draw was offering wonderful encouragement to those still left in it, whatever their ranking, this was surely it.

That obviously added, therefore, to the excited fascination surrounding the match between Tim Henman and Luke Milligan for, apart from guaranteeing the presence of a British player in the bottom half for the fourth round, it was the first time since Bunny Austin had played Eric Filby 58 years earlier that two Englishmen had faced each other in singles on the Centre Court.

Opposite: Boris Becker winces from the pain after the injury to his right forearm which forced him to default against South African Neville Godwin (below).

Tim Henman (previous pages) was well on his way to beating Luke Milligan before steady drizzle delayed his progress overnight but MaliVai Washington (below) beat the weather by dropping only six games against Bohdan Ulihrach.

With Henman, who had been even higher, now at 62 in the rankings and Milligan still in that modest making-up-the-numbers range at 278, few expected the result to be in doubt even though, by courtesy of the rain, at least the teenager can say it was not until more than 19 hours after they started that he was beaten.

Henman, 21, made a spectacular start. There was a roar of appreciation as well as delight from the crowd when he produced a brilliant, ripping backhand down the line on the second point and, having broken to love, he then held to love just to emphasise his superiority. Indeed he dropped only two points on his first five service games when Milligan, in all fairness, was needing time to overcome stage nerves.

Just when Henman was ready to serve for the match at 6–1, 6–3, 5–4, having recovered from 0–3 in the third set, the drizzle, which had sent players off court for 25 minutes in earlier matches, began again. It was 5.25 p.m. and although everyone waited around for almost another two hours in the hope of a resumption, not another ball was hit on the day.

Only two third-round men's singles matches had been completed, MaliVai Washington overwhelming Bohdan Ulihrach of the Czech Republic and Sweden's Thomas Johansson bringing to an end a memorable week for Andre Agassi's conqueror, Doug Flach, 6–1, 6–4, 6–3.

The first rain delay could not have come at a worse time for them. When they returned only two more points had to be played.

Ironically about an hour before Becker was in trouble on No. 1 Court, Arantxa Sanchez Vicario, the other runner-up from the singles the year before, was causing consternation on Centre Court when she too was having trouble with her wrist.

Fortunately for the Spaniard – and, indeed, for Wimbledon this year – the problem was not so serious as it initially seemed and she comfortably won her match against Japan's Naoko Sawamatsu.

When the arm injury first became obvious towards the end of the first set, it looked threatening. Sanchez called for the trainer, took an injury timeout before serving for the first set and clearly winced in pain after hitting forehands for a while.

'I stretched one of the ligaments in my arm,' she said. 'I went for a shot but my wrist went the other way so I stretched it. It was painful when I was serving and when I hit hard shots but I'm having treatment and, with a couple of days off now, I should be fine next week.'

Next in line for Sanchez would be Sabine Appelmans, 24 and ranked 28th in the world, who continued the upsets of the seeds by defeating Brenda Schultz-McCarthy from Holland 7–5, 3–6, 12–10. For Schultz-McCarthy, the 11th seed, it was another of her erratic days. She hit 13 aces but also 14 double faults, the last of them at the start of what proved to be the decisive game. The Dutch player saved four match points but finally yielded when Appelmans passed her with a backhand down the line.

Mary Joe Fernandez, the ninth seed, continued her impressively smooth progress through the first week by outclassing the Argentinian, Florencia Labat, 6–2, 6–0. On a busy day for the trainers, Gigi Fernandez, the Wimbledon doubles champion three times with Natasha Zvereva, also needed treatment on the court. She damaged her right shoulder and for a while lay spreadeagled on Court No. 3 while receiving physiotherapy. Fernandez was able to continue but was beaten 6–2, 7–5 by Judith Wiesner.

Arantxa Sanchez Vicario (below) needed treatment for a strained wrist before joining Mary Joe Fernandez (right) in the last 16 of the ladies' singles.

WIMBLEDON

day 6

SATURDAY 29 JUNE

Wayne Ferreira recovered from two sets down but then did not have enough left for the fifth as Magnus Gustafsson (opposite) went through to be Tim Henman's next challenger.

Seldom has so much attention been paid to just five points on the Centre Court as during the two minutes seven seconds it took Tim Henman to serve out the one game he still needed when rain stopped play the night before to complete a 6–1, 6–3, 6–4 defeat of Luke Milligan.

On the first of them Henman dropped a simple volley into the net but then came two service-based winners and two errors from an outclassed opponent – and he was free to concentrate on trying to become the first British player since Roger Taylor in 1973 to reach the quarter-finals.

According to the seedings, South African Wayne Ferreira should have become Henman's next challenger. And when he raced into a 5–2 first-set lead with two breaks against Magnus Gustafsson on Court 13, everything seemed to be going to plan.

In a year, though, when the seedings were notoriously undermined by a combination of lack of commitment in some cases, brilliant performances in others and injuries first to Thomas Muster and then to Boris Becker, Ferreira joined the lengthy list of victims. The frustration was evident, not only when he was questioning calls as the first-set lead slipped away – and then the second set as well – and although he levelled things at two sets all, a break for 3–1 in the fifth again undermined his resolve.

Gustafsson, ranked 37 in the world and picking up his game after serious shoulder and foot injuries in the previous two years after making it to the top ten in the summer of 1991, was the eighth player to beat a seed in the men's singles at Wimbledon '96 and Australian Patrick Rafter, also fresh and eager on one of his favourite surfaces after injury, joined the list with his 4–6, 6–3, 4–6, 6–1, 6–3 defeat of Marc Rosset, seeded 14.

Rafter looked like a man thrilled to be playing the game again after a difficult time recovering from a wrist injury which eventually needed surgery and he frequently ran from his chair after changeovers to the baseline and refused to be deflected by the forehand errors which more or less handed 6ft 7in Rosset the third set. A superb lob helped Rafter break in the opening game of the fifth set and again two games later as that familiar

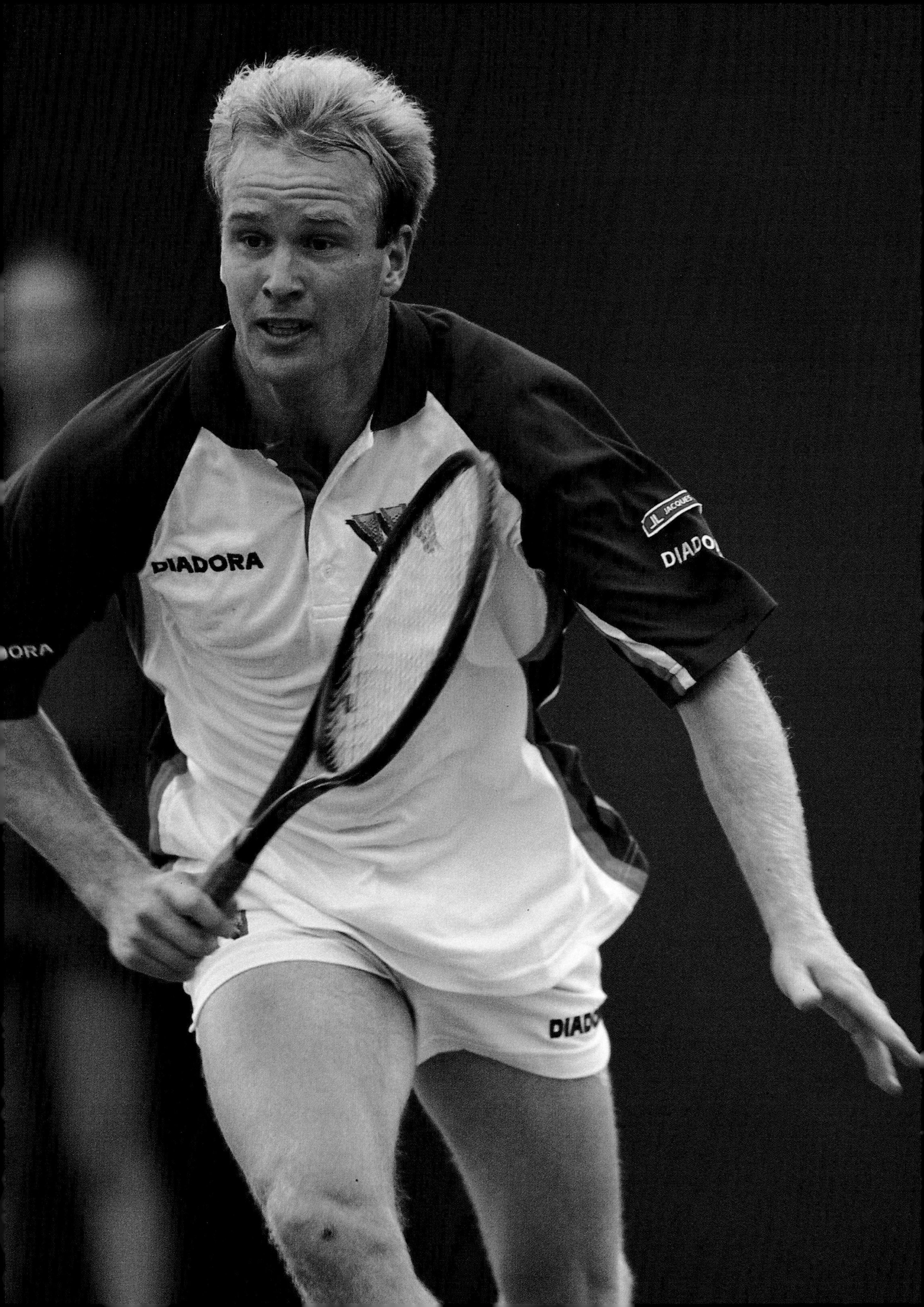
DIADORA
JACQUES

goofy grin on the Swiss player's face was replaced by bewildered despair.

Elsewhere in the men's singles Michael Stich dropped a set against Sandon Stolle but won well enough 6–3, 4–6, 6–2, 6–3 and then put the blame for there being four seeds remaining in the top half of the draw and only one in the bottom on the seeding committee. 'I really think they should look at the way they are doing things right now,' said the 1991 champion, presumably forgetting that after the top two seeds have been placed at the top and bottom of the draw, the others, in pairs, all draw to see if they go into the top half or the bottom. In other words the draw rather than the seeds is what counts most.

Todd Martin, down 5–2 in the first set, rallied to beat Italy's Renzo Furlan 7–6, 6–4, 6–2 to emerge as the only seed in the bottom half of the draw and then defended the way things had worked out. 'I think it's nice to see new names and for the players concerned it's great, for they will never have experienced something like this before.' Whether he felt the same way after what was to happen to him in the semi-finals is another matter.

Altogether Richard Krajicek, Rafter, Jason Stoltenberg, Henman, Gustafsson (who, like Henman, had never gone beyond the second round before), Swedish newcomer Thomas Johansson, Paul Haarhuis, MaliVai Washington, Alexander Radulescu and South African qualifier Neville Godwin, the beneficiary of Boris Becker's injury, were in the last 16 for the first time.

So by the end of a marathon near-nine-hour day on some courts, Wimbledon was left with only five seeds in the men's singles, the lowest on record in a year when there have been 16, rather than eight seeds. Briefly one feared that there might be another, far more significant scalp to be won. For after sailing through the opening two sets comfortably enough, defending champion Pete Sampras started to wobble against the Slovakian, Karol Kucera. Although he rallied from 3–5 to 5–5 in the tie-break with a magnificent

low dipping return when a shot of that calibre was needed, Sampras not only missed a simple backhand volley when facing set point at 5–6 but, even more ominously, was rubbing his back.

For the next three games, as he went to 0–3, Sampras's lack of mobility added to the concern that back problems, well

Opposite: An exultant Pat Rafter underlined his return to form and, more especially, fitness, by upsetting Marc Rosset (inset).

Alexander Radulescu (below) surged to another five-sets victory, this time over David Wheaton, as the German media started to take notice of their Romanian import.

Mixed feelings for two Germans.
Below: Anke Huber's stomach upset left her
struggling against Japan's Ai Sugiyama
(bottom) but Steffi Graf (opposite) took
only 41 minutes to trounce Nicole Arendt.

documented in his record in the past, were returning to inhibit him. Yet suddenly, on his first chance to break back in the seventh game, Sampras made a desperate dash forward to return a drop shot as a winner and Kucera's head dropped.

The fourth set went to a tie-break but the Slovakian, who had been serving so strongly and even shown a willingness to come in and put away first volleys, suffered a cruel net cord at 3–4, double-faulted at 3–5 and was then passed for the match-winner at 3–6.

One more seed was knocked out in the women's singles but, as with Becker, there were extenuating circumstances for an unlucky German, Anke Huber, the fifth seed. Trailing 5–6, she had to send for the trainer, who gave her some pills to try and ease a stomach upset. With Japan's 29th-ranked Ai Sugiyama stretching her from side to side, however, Huber was in no state either to resist or to be able to take the initiative herself and, having lost the first-set tie-break 7–3, the second set raced away from her 6–1.

Steffi Graf, wearing a patch just below the right knee which had troubled her again in her previous match, provided the Centre Court crowd with an early shock, losing the first eight points against Nicole Arendt. You could easily sense the feelings of foreboding spread-

ing round the arena at the end of a week in which so many of the best-known names had been forced out of the tournament in various ways.

Then, just as spectacularly as she had been missing shots in those first two games, Graf began hitting powerfully athletic winners at will. Less than 15 minutes after she had been 0–2, the first set was hers 6–2 for the loss of only seven more points. The reigning champion was clearly delighted at the way her forehand was producing so many explosive winners and, having taken six games in succession to win the first set, she then took five in a row from 1–1 to win the second. Although Graf double-faulted twice when she reached two match points at 5–1, 40–15, this was a matter for mirth, rather than concern. It was all over in 41 minutes, leaving Graf happily relaxed when she and coach Heinz Guenthardt went out later to beat the Australians, Andrew Florent and Catherine Barclay, 6–1, 7–5 in the first round of the mixed doubles.

Graf's next opponent would be Martina Hingis, the 15-year-old Swiss miss, who beat the American, Linda Wild, 6–3, 2–6, 6–1. When they last met, at the Italian Open in Rome in May, the teenager won but, as she recognised, 'playing Steffi on grass will be something entirely different'.

Once the rain stopped the umbrellas went down and there were smiling faces all around to celebrate Tim Henman's victory over Magnus Gustafsson (inset), which took him into the quarter-finals.

Not even the frequent interruptions on a day when the expertise of the court coverers, almost redundant for the three previous years, came into its own diminished the patriotism on Centre Court where a British player reached the quarter-finals for the first time since Roger Taylor in 1973.

Tim Henman, 21, a year younger than Fred Perry, Britain's last champion, when he reached the quarter-finals for the first time in 1931, succeeded where Jeremy Bates (twice), Andrew Foster and Greg Rusedski had all lost in the four preceding years, by winning his fourth-round match 7–6, 6–4, 7–6 against Sweden's Magnus Gustafsson.

While not matching the consistent high quality of his first-round form against Yevgeny Kafelnikov, especially on first serves, and although Gustafsson, for all the power in his serve, full-swing forehands and double-fisted backhands, never seemed quite sure whether to come in or stay back on grass, it was another magnificent effort by Henman.

Five times the players had to walk on to the court. Five times the nerves must have been churning in the stomach but through it all Henman demonstrated a coolness and match temperament which meant he was never driven more than slightly off his intended course, and when he was, the speed and effectiveness with which he took corrective action provided everyone not Swedish with additional excitement.

When the two men first walked on to court at 2.47 p.m., with time only for Gustafsson to win the toss and decide that Henman should serve first before the rain forced them to walk off again, such was the welcome from the crowd, several of them waving either Union Jacks or the flag of St George, that it briefly – and possibly significantly – distracted Sabine Appelmans at a key moment of her match against Arantxa Sanchez Vicario, on No. 1 Court.

Each time Henman and Gustafsson returned after that, first to begin playing at 3.13 p.m., for 23 minutes, then at

4.13 p.m. when they never got beyond knocking up, again at 4.49 p.m. for another 19 minutes and finally at 6.13 when they were able to play through to the finish at 7.45 p.m., the scale of the welcome inevitably became more modest. Henman, however, only had to strike his first winner in each period of play for total enthusiasm to be rekindled and at the end the reception was rapturous and prolonged. It had after all been a long wait, in more ways than one.

Henman was not even born the last time Britain had a quarter-finalist in the men's singles and yet here was one who, according to Gustafsson later, 'probably wouldn't be able to live with a Sampras or an Ivanisevic in the final but as for whether he could get there, why not?'

The match lasted one minute under two hours but when victory came it was almost five hours after they had first attempted to start. Many might have buckled beneath the frustration of so many delays but not Henman, whose mental as well as physical resilience was now becoming such an asset. 'It was just his day. He played better on the big points and kept his nerve throughout,' said Gustafsson.

Henman could not have wished for a better start – an ace on the first point, then a break, albeit not until the fifth chance, when his opponent served for the first time – but then a seventh game in which he hardly managed a first serve meant the initiative had been lost and the British number one's resolve was immediately being put to the test. It was not found wanting.

The first set went to a tie-break which Henman won 7–2, starting and ending with aces and in between forcing an error from Gustafsson, who stayed back when he should probably have come in on the second point, and then taking a 5–1 lead with another of those stinging, full-blooded forehands which can be match-winners.

In the second set Gustafsson led 3–0 but Henman broke back to 2–3 with a Becker-style diving forehand volley and

'I was prepared for the way the crowd would be cheering for Tim and I think they were great. It is one thing if the crowd are annoying you but the crowd was fair. It was a great atmosphere. I liked it. I enjoyed it. I wish we had a Wimbledon in Sweden.'

Magnus Gustafsson after his defeat by Tim Henman.

Todd Martin's double-handed backhands (opposite) served him well against Thomas Johansson, but well though Patrick Rafter (below) served and volleyed, he could not match Goran Ivanisevic's brilliant form on the day.

went on to break again in the ninth game to lead 5–4 when the Swede, from 15–0, made four simple errors, including a double fault, as if his uncertainty as to how to play on grass was too much for him at that moment.

Henman served out for the set and in the third all went with serve until the eighth game when too many missed first serves allowed Gustafsson to break and look seemingly poised at least to force a fourth set. 'Too often I wasn't going for my first serve enough – and then going for my second serve a little too much,' said Henman. 'I wasn't quite getting the balance right between the two.'

Not that that concerned him when Gustafsson was serving for the set for it reached 15–40 and Henman then broke back with a wonderful backhand pass steered down the line. Three games later, having broken again for 6–5, Henman served for the match, only for that lack of balance between first and second serves to strike again so that once more a tie-breaker was necessary.

Henman made the ideal start, keeping Gustafsson on the run until opening up the space for a winning volley and a mini-break on the first point. A brilliant backhand drop-shot volley off a really testing dipping return increased Henman's lead to 3–0 and then it was as much as the crowd could do to stifle their joy when the Swede double-faulted to make it 4–0. At 6–2 Henman had four match points.

On the first he missed a service return. On the second there was a false alarm for the celebrations when what looked to have been an ace was called a 'let', but when the point restarted Henman was quickly to the net, only to snatch at a backhand volley. When it came to the third match point, however, Gustafsson made one of his windmill swings but mistimed his return and the ball flew wide. The euphoria was everywhere.

As after the Kafelnikov, Danny Sapsford and Luke Milligan wins, though, Henman was keeping his feet firmly on the floor, merely saying how pleased he

was to be in the last eight and, hopefully, that there was 'still a lot more tennis to play'.

Whether that would be against 13th seed Todd Martin or another Swede, Thomas Johansson, remained undecided. Their match had been switched to Court Six after the weather delayed the original programme so severely, and

when bad light stopped play Martin, who had been a set and 0–40 down in the first game of the second, was leading 3–6, 6–3, 7–5.

Only three of the eight scheduled matches in the fourth round of the men's singles were completed. On Court No. 2, Goran Ivanisevic resisted a thrilling serve-and-volley challenge from Aus-tralian Patrick Rafter for a 7–6, 4–6, 7–6, 6–1 victory spread over two hours 24 minutes' playing time and the best part of another four hours lost because of the rain delays. Rafter saved a break point in the opening game but not until Ivanisevic had taken a two-sets-to-one lead by winning a crucial third-set tie-break 9–7 did he have to face another.

Round 1	Round 2	Round 3
Miss J. WARD	Miss C. TAYLOR	Miss M. PIERCE
Miss C. TAYLOR	6-3 6-2	6-4 6-2
Miss R. HIRAKI	Miss R. HIRAKI	v
Miss C. SINGER	7-5 6-4	
Miss C. MORARIU	Miss N. MEDVEDEVA	Miss N. MEDVEDEVA
Miss N. MEDVEDEVA	5-7 7-5 6-4	6-3 6-2
Miss E. LIKHOVTSEVA	Miss E. LIKHOVTSEVA	
Miss E.S.H. CALLENS	7-6 6-3	
Miss A. GAVALDON	Miss K. ADAMS	Miss E. LIKHOVTSEVA
Miss K.M. ADAMS	7-6 6-1	6-4 6-3
Mrs L. NEILAND	Mrs L. NEILAND	v
Miss K.S. RINALDI STUNKEL	6-3 6-3	
Miss M. SCHNELL	Miss L.A. DAVENPORT	Mrs L. NEILAND
Miss L.A. DAVENPORT	6-4 6-1	6-3 6-2
Miss K. HABSUDOVA	Miss J. WIESNER	
Mrs J.K. WIESNER	6-0 7-5	
Mrs M. WERDEL WITMEYER	Miss M. PAZ	Miss J. WIESNER
Miss M. PAZ	6-4 6-4	6-2 6-3
Miss K. NOWAK	Miss G. PIZZICHINI	v
Miss G. PIZZICHINI	6-0 6-2	
Miss T. JECMENICA	Miss G. FERNANDEZ	Miss G. FERNANDEZ
Miss G. FERNANDEZ	2-6 6-3 6-4	6-2 6-1
Miss R. ZRUBAKOVA	Miss S-H. PARK	
Miss S-H. PARK	6-2 6-2	
Miss A. FRAZIER	Miss A. FRAZIER	Miss A. FRAZIER
Miss D. RANDRIANTEFY	6-3 6-1	6-4 6-1
Miss I. GORROCHATEGUI	Miss I. GORROCHATEGUI	v
Miss A. SMASHNOVA	6-4 7-5	
Miss S. SMITH	Miss I. SPIRLEA	Miss I. GORROCHATEGUI
Miss I. SPIRLEA 15	3-6 6-1 6-2	6-3 2-6 6-4
Mrs B. SCHULTZ-McCARTHY 11	Miss B. SCHULTZ-McCARTHY	
Miss J. KRUGER	6-0 6-3	
Miss R. BOBKOVA	Miss J. WATANABE	Mrs B. SCHULTZ-McCARTH
Miss J. WATANABE	6-3 6-3	6-3 6-0
Miss A. OLSZA	Miss A. OLSZA	v
Miss M. GRZYBOWSKA	6-4 6-4	
Miss N. MIYAGI	Miss S. APPLEMANS	Miss S. APPLEMANS
Miss S. APPELMANS	6-3 6-4	6-3 6-1
Miss F. PERFETTI	Miss F. PERFETTI	
Mrs M. SANCHEZ LORENZO	4-6 6-2 11-9	
Miss N. SAWAMATSU	Miss N. SAWAMATSU	Miss N. SAWAMATSU
Miss N.K. KIJIMUTA	7-6 6-2	6-4 6-0
Miss M. OREMANS	Miss M. OREMANS	v
Miss R. GRANDE	7-6 6-3	
Miss A. SERRA-ZANETTI	Miss A. SANCHEZ VICARIO	Miss A. SANCHEZ VICARIO
Miss A. SANCHEZ VICARIO 4	6-3 6-4	7-5 6-3
Miss A. HUBER 5	Miss A. HUBER	
Miss G. LEON GARCIA	6-1 6-1	
Miss P.H. SHRIVER	Miss P.H. SHRIVER	Miss A. HUBER
Miss A. ELLWOOD	6-4 6-4	6-2 6-1
Miss K. GODRIDGE	Miss H. SUKOVA	v
Miss H. SUKOVA	6-3 6-3	
Miss A. KREMER	Miss A. SUGIYAMA	Miss A. SUGIYAMA
Miss A. SUGIYAMA	7-5 6-4	6-4 6-1
Miss P. BEGEROW	Miss B. SCHETT	
Miss B. SCHETT	4-6 6-2 6-3	
Miss F. LABAT	Miss F. LABAT	Miss F. LABAT
Mrs T.S. WHITLINGER JONES	6-1 2-6 7-5	6-2 2-6 6-2
Miss S. CACIC	Miss S. TESTUD	
Miss S. TESTUD	6-1 6-3	
Miss J. KANDARR	Miss M.J. FERNANDEZ	Miss M.J. FERNANDEZ

Miss M. PIERCE
6-4 6-1

v

Miss E. LIKHOVTSEVA
6-3 4-6 6-0

Miss J. WIESNER
6-2 7-5

v

Miss A. FRAZIER
6-0 6-3

v

Miss S. APPLEMANS
7-5 3-6 12-10

v

Miss A. SANCHEZ VICARIO
6-4 6-1

Miss A. SUGIYAMA
7-6 6-1

v

Miss M.J. FERNANDEZ
6-2 6-0

Previous pages: Keeping up to date with progress in the ladies' singles.

Martina Hingis (below) enjoyed herself even in defeat by Steffi Graf (bottom).

Rafter saved three set points from 3–6 in the third-set tie-break and then had a set point of his own on serve at 7–6 but the Croatian, also playing with surprisingly sustained concentration, responded with the shot of the match – a double-handed cross-court backhand which seemed to break his opponent's spirit.

At least there was some Australian delight. Jason Stoltenberg beat Switzerland's Jakob Hlasek 6–2, 7–6, 6–2. Thankfully for those in the referee's office, the eight matches to decide the quarter-final line-up a day later in the women's singles were completed, even though that also involved the judicious movement of the Jana Novotna–Patricia Hy-Boulais match, which should originally have followed Ivanisevic and Rafter. Novotna, obviously content not to have been so delayed, won 6–3, 6–1 to earn another crack at Steffi Graf, who in turn had comfortably beaten Martina Hingis 6–1, 6–4 in the first match on Centre Court, to avenge her defeat by the 15-year-old Swiss prodigy at the Italian Open two months earlier.

Graf was clearly determined to stamp her authority on the match as quickly as possible and, despite a double fault on the first point, certainly did that. After just nine minutes she led 4–0, with her renowned forehand on full power. Hingis had a chance in the sixth game of the second set with two break points when she was leading 3–2 but the German saved one and Hingis wasted the other with a loose forehand which floated wide.

Arantxa Sanchez Vicario, narrowly beaten by Graf in a thrilling final a year earlier, kept on course for a possible repeat meeting when she recovered from losing the first set to beat Belgium's Sabine Appelmans 3–6, 6–2, 6–1. Appelmans broke the Sanchez serve in the first game of the first and second sets and even outrallied the Spaniard until suddenly, at 0–2 in the second set, the fourth seed started to become more adventurous, in addition to her customary scuttling to retrieve at the back of the court.

Then, facing a break point at 2–2, Appelmans was about to serve when she was forced to stop, distracted by the tumultuous reception being given to Henman when he walked out for the first time on the adjoining Centre Court. When the noise died down Appelmans tried again but double-faulted. Sanchez went on to take eleven consecutive games on the way to her 3–6, 6–2, 6–1 win.

Mary Joe Fernandez also dropped a set in her rain-interrupted match with

the unseeded Ai Sugiyama of Japan but Mary Pierce was in seventh heaven after playing so resourcefully on a surface still largely foreign to her to reach the quarter-finals 6–2, 6–3 against Elena Likhovtseva. By contrast Conchita Martinez, the 1994 champion, despite winning the first set, looked anything but happy as she made many of the unforced errors and lost a long and undistinguished match to 12th-seeded Kimiko Date. The first two games were played between rain breaks, which did not help, and the frequent cheers from the Henman match left the crowd in no doubt that something more entertaining was going on next door.

Martinez rallied from 0–3 in the second set but then lost it in the tie-break and thereafter she subsided somewhat limply, so much so that even Date, though overjoyed to have won, said it did not mean so much to her as beating Graf in the Fed Cup.

Long shadows cast over one of the outside courts as play continues well into the evening.

Hard though she tried, Jana Novotna was unable to trouble defending champion Steffi Graf as much as usual on this occasion.

The weather problems the day before meant the ladies did not have the main stage all to themselves for the quarter-finals but, if not particularly memorable matches, at least they provided as many talking points as those involving the men. Steffi Graf raced through to meet Kimiko Date in one semi-final and Arantxa Sanchez Vicario comfortably qualified to meet the unseeded Meredith McGrath in the other.

On paper the opening match on Centre Court between Graf and Jana Novotna ought to have been one to cherish. After all, although Graf had won all but three of their previous 27 clashes, many of them had been close enough to be exciting and their 1993 Wimbledon final, when Novotna served and had a point for 5–1 in the final set, was a classic.

This time, however, it was surprisingly and disappointingly straightforward, partly because Novotna was either unwilling or unable to play the normal aggressive, risk-taking tennis which is her forte and which she must do to stand any chance of breaking Graf's control, but more particularly because the defending champion's illustrious forehand was again in sparkling form.

'It was a lot easier than I expected,' said Graf after her 6–3, 6–2 success in 61 minutes, 'but I returned really well right from the beginning and that gave me a positive feeling. She knew she had to do something better, such as playing closer to the lines and as a result made mistakes.'

Novotna had one of those days when she seemed unsure about when to come in, which was a rare enough occurrence in the first set, while both her groundstrokes and later her volleys too often landed in mid-court, giving Graf the chance to move forward and slam winners off the top of the bounce.

After Graf double-faulted to be broken when she served for the first set at 5–1, someone in the crowd shouted, 'Come on, Jana, don't let the Germans win again' – a reference to their success in the European soccer championships at

Wembley a few days earlier. Both players grinned but Graf remained unruffled.

It was Graf's 31st win in 33 matches this year but next she would be meeting one of the two players who had beaten her along the way, Kimiko Date, the first Japanese woman to reach a semi-final of the singles at The Championships. Date is one of those players who, despite looking lightweight, is still difficult to put away. She can extend rallies long enough until she either has the chance to place a winner with delicate, rather than pounding skill, or the opponent makes a mistake. In her quarter-final against Mary Pierce, seeded 13, one place below her, it was a case of both and increasingly the latter when the French number one suddenly seemed to 'freeze' after taking the first set.

When Pierce, regal from the back of the court and occasionally imperious with her touches at the net, took the opening set 6–3 on a rasping forehand winner and then a brilliant double-handed backhand drop shot, she looked well set for her first Wimbledon semi-final. Instead both her tennis and her nerve went into a disastrous decline. A modest match became a really shoddy one amid the many errors but full marks to Date, still savouring her Fed Cup triumph over Graf in Tokyo in April, for plodding along to a 3–6, 6–3, 6–1 victory, albeit with much unintended assistance from the other side of the net.

Arantxa Sanchez Vicario overcame a terrible start to beat Austria's unseeded Judith Wiesner 6–4, 6–0. The outcome was always predictable once the Spaniard grabbed the first set but at least Wiesner had the consolation of winning the best point of the match. It lasted 28 strokes and included everything from drives and lobs to drop shots and volleys, not to mention much scurrying along the baseline to keep the rally going, until Sanchez lost her first set point by just missing the baseline.

Monica Seles had originally been expected to come through as the semi-final rival for Sanchez but after her dismissal

Kimiko Date turns and signals her delight to friends in the players' box after reaching the semi-finals when her steadiness left Mary Pierce (below) agonisingly frustrated as too many unforced errors crept into her game.

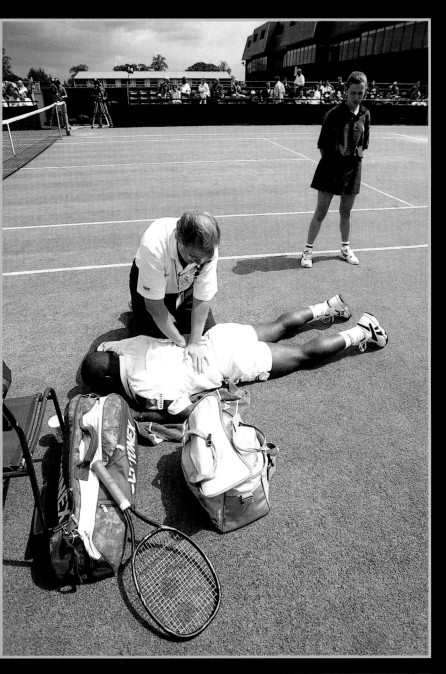

Trainer Bill Norris applies emergency treatment to MaliVai Washington for a back injury which briefly threatened the American's run of success, but the mood is more light-hearted as Jonathan Stark and Martina Navratilova (above) continue their defence of the mixed doubles title. Meanwhile former world number one Tracy Austin (left) kept American television viewers up to date with events on Centre Court.

Cedric Pioline's backhand let him down a little too often as he was outclassed by Pete Sampras (opposite), whose own backhand was in fine fettle on the day.

another American was expected to take her place. That was true – but not the American one had imagined it would be. Mary Joe Fernandez, seeded nine, ricked her back while practising with her coach Harold Solomon in the morning and her mobility was clearly inhibited as she was beaten 6–3, 6–1 by the unseeded, Swiss-based Meredith McGrath. Injury or no injury to Fernandez, however, McGrath, a recognised grass-court player who had won Eastbourne in 1994 after beating Martina Navratilova along the way and Birmingham two weeks before Wimbledon, was overjoyed.

McGrath, ranked 27 in the world, could scarcely believe what she had achieved. When she arrived in the interview room she announced, 'I only just stopped shaking about five minutes ago. It's an honour to be in the semis at Wimbledon. I'm just thrilled to be here and to be playing the kind of tennis I am. Coming into the tournament it never crossed my mind. I was just hoping to win my first round.' As for the heavy strapping on her right thigh which suggested that like Fernandez she had also had physical problems, she explained that she had been wearing the strapping for some time and said, 'It's nothing major.'

McGrath was the only unseeded player to reach the semi-finals but among the men it was already known there would be at least four and possibly six in the quarter-finals and the guarantee of at least one in the semi-finals. In the event five made it to the last eight including the least likely, 21-year-old Alexander Radulescu, a German born in Romania, playing his first Grand Slam, who, when the entry list closed, had a ranking which meant he was the very last player to be given a place.

Coming into Wimbledon Radulescu's ranking had improved to 91 but for all that, just as Tim Henman had hardly become known outside Britain before this tournament, so few in Britain had ever heard of this 6ft 2in, strapping young man who had worked harder than most

to stay in the race. He was equally anonymous to many of his own fellow countrymen, among them their Davis Cup captain, Niki Pilic. It was hardly surprising. Radulescu made little impact as a junior, mainly because of injuries. Like so many in the modern game, the serve is a prime weapon in Radulescu's armoury and after adding ten more aces during his 6–3, 6–0, 6–4 defeat of South African qualifier Neville Godwin, the beneficiary of Boris Becker's injury, he took his total to 101, nine ahead of everyone else.

To reach the fourth round, Radulescu, who began by beating the 15th-seeded Frenchman, Arnaud Boetsch, had won three consecutive five-set matches, something which had been achieved only three times before at Wimbledon during the Open era since 1968 – Jan Kodes in 1974, Russell Simpson in 1982 and Todd Martin (ominously enough, perhaps, for Tim Henman) in 1994.

His straightforward defeat of Godwin would bring him up against the equally unseeded MaliVai Washington, who beat Dutchman Paul Haarhuis, also unseeded, with a typically efficient, well-balanced display of attacking tactics to become the third American in the last eight.

He joined Pete Sampras and Martin, the last player to have beaten the world champion on grass at the Stella Artois tournament at Queen's Club in 1994, who completed his match unfinished the night before against Sweden's Thomas Johansson, 3–6, 6–3, 7–5, 6–2, in readiness to face Henman who, curiously enough, he also beat at Queen's Club that year.

Sampras reinforced the belief that it would take something and someone rather special to ruin his dream of a fourth consecutive title (which was to prove the case) with the way he outclassed Frenchman Cedric Pioline 6–4, 6–4, 6–2. He is seldom more dangerous than when apparently under threat and that was demonstrated once again when, having broken for 3–2 in the second set, he was

Former men's singles champion Michael Stich was unable to stem the flood of heavy-artillery winners from Holland's Richard Krajicek (opposite).

15–40 on his own serve after Pioline produced a sensational running backhand down the line, which prompted a cry of 'encore' from the crowd.

The strident Sampras response was to produce two service winners and an ace on his next three points. The only threat he faced after that was when at the end of the first game of the third set, chasing a shot close to the net but out wide near the umpire's chair, he could have been injured. He leapt over a chair and slid on to the box where the new balls are kept. 'I had only one place to go,' he said. 'I kind of tweaked my back a bit but it's not too bad,' he added, having proved it by then taking the next eleven points.

Richard Krajicek, who would be next in line for Sampras, had additional reason for celebration after his 6–4, 7–6, 6–4 defeat of tenth-seeded Michael Stich, for despite a world ranking of 14, the 6ft 5in heavy-serving Krajicek was surprised and possibly a shade unlucky not to have been seeded. Not that he was making a big deal of it. When Thomas Muster, who would have been the seventh seed, withdrew, the Dutchman, as the highest-ranked unseeded competitor, moved into his position in the draw – but without the status to go with it.

'I could understand it a bit but in the end I proved them wrong,' said Krajicek, at last free from the shoulder problems which have dogged him in the past, and he dropped only four points in five service games in the first set. He also hit 13 aces, including one in the ninth game of the match which was struck with such ferocity that Stich dived out of the way.

Stich's only chance to turn things round came when he had a break point in both the first and third games of the second set but, once again, Krajicek's serve was dominant, with a service winner and an ace to save them.

Meanwhile the doubles events were beginning to take shape, not least in the mixed, where, partnered by Jonathan Stark, Martina Navratilova was beginning a bid for a 20th Wimbledon title which would enable her to draw level with Billie Jean King's record. A large crowd on No. 2 Court watched them beat Andrew Kratzmann, brother of Mark, and Sweden's Maria Lindstrom 6–3, 3–6, 6–2. 'I was really nervous. My knees were knocking,' said Navratilova. 'I was so thrilled to be out there I can't believe I'm back again.'

Late in the evening after an injured Heinz Guenthardt had been forced to abort plans to partner Steffi Graf, the cheers rang loud and long in response to a thrilling cut-and-thrust contest – the best of the day on Centre Court – as Pat Cash and Mary Pierce just outlasted Menno Oosting of Holland and Els Callens from Belgium 6–2, 5–7, 8–6.

WIMBLEDON

day **9**

WEDNESDAY 3 JULY

Congratulations! Martina Navratilova and a host of other players joined Sir Cliff Richard when he entertained the crowd with an impromptu singing-in-the-rain concert, to help while away the time before the clouds parted and the tennis could continue on Day Nine.

Sadly, the weather forecasters who had thankfully been fooled by the elements the day before when they suggested the court covers would be on more than they were off, were all too accurate with their prediction that this would be another day for anoraks and umbrellas.

Although the first shots were struck at 12.37 p.m. and the last at 8.30 p.m., in the meantime there had been three lengthy rain breaks which meant that not one of the four men's singles quarter-finals due to be decided had been completed and two of them, including Tim Henman v. Todd Martin, which almost everyone in Britain, it seemed, was eager to follow, had not even got on court.

Henman, who had been practising with Luke Milligan, his fellow British player whom he beat in the third round, when Pete Sampras and Richard Krajicek walked out on to Centre Court and Jason Stoltenberg began what was to become a thrilling assault on Goran Ivani-sevic's status as fourth seed, spent most of the afternoon either playing backgammon with LTA coach Peter Fleming, John McEnroe's former triumphant Wimbledon doubles partner, or sleeping in the locker room.

At the end of a frustrating day, however, the crowds, both on Centre and No. 1 Courts, could look back on some spectacular, albeit indecisive tennis, with Sampras, the defending champion, two sets down to Krajicek and Ivanise-vic clinging on, two sets to one down after saving a match point at 4–5 in the third set in spectacular fashion against the Australian.

For some, no doubt, even more rewarding than the tennis was the impromptu concert provided by Sir Cliff Richard, a member of the All England Club, during the three hours 40 minutes afternoon disruption to play, on the Centre Court.

After three years with no need for any other form of entertainment, the servicemen and women and the police once again launched into sing-songs etc. which helped warm the spirits, if not the

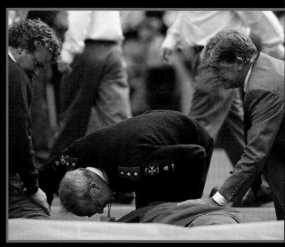

Brilliant serving by Richard Krajicek (opposite) left Pete Sampras with plenty to ponder on this rainy day when one of the groundstaff was injured as the court covers went on and off and, over on No. 1 Court, Goran Ivanisevic (above) found himself close to defeat against Jason Stoltenberg.

It looks good but, although Goran Ivanisevic snatched the third set to keep the match alive, he was the one who eventually finished with his tail between his legs.

form of music, there was another . . . and another . . . as many of those who had left their seats hurried back. Then, led by Pam Shriver (who else?), a few players appeared to provide one of Britain's most enduringly popular entertainers with a backing group including former champions Conchita Martinez, Virginia Wade and finally, welcomed by another huge cheer, Martina Navratilova.

Journalists and spectators from other countries could not believe it. It was one of those wonderfully glorious and unexpected occasions, of which there have been many over the years, that could probably only happen at Wimbledon, even though Wimbledon has the worldwide reputation of being the last place where it would be *allowed* to happen. No one who was there, or watched on television, will forget the scene in a hurry, especially Cpl Lorna Waud, whom he persuaded to join him for one song.

'It was a wonderful experience, one of the best in my life,' said Sir Cliff, who added, 'I never thought I would ever have a chance to play on the Centre Court.' It was the perfect final touch and timing when, during a rousing rendition of 'Congratulations', the tent over the Centre Court started to be lowered and the players were preparing to resume the tennis. As actress Joanna Lumley, watching from the stands, might have said, it was 'Absolutely Fabulous'.

Sampras and Krajicek, who had reached 2–2 in the first set before the rain, including a wonderful third game of nine deuces and 12 minutes when the Dutchman saved five break points, all created by the American's subtle, rather than powered returns, began again at 4.37 p.m. and continued until 5.09 p.m. By then Krajicek, now serving magnificently, had taken the set 7–5 after breaking in the 12th game with first a stunning backhand down the line and then an equally impressive forehand return, hit from his backhand corner.

He was also 2–1 ahead on serve in the second.

A further delay of one hour 37 min-

bodies, of those huddled under umbrellas on Centre and No. 1 Court. Then, on Centre Court, Tony Adamson from BBC Radio again started interviewing personalities such as former British player John Lloyd over the public address system.

Suddenly Sir Cliff Richard joined in, answering a plea from Christopher Gorringe, Chief Executive of the All England Club, to take part. He could not have done so with greater enthusiasm – and enjoyment. As they say in the theatre, 'the show must go on.' Persuaded to sing one song, 'Summer Holiday', despite not having his guitar with him or any other utes was followed by another 51 minutes of play in which Sampras saved a set point at 5–6 with a backhand volley perilously close to the line before Krajicek then opened up a two-sets lead by taking the tie-break 7–3, helped by another two aces and a crucial Sampras double fault on the third point.

It was 1–1 in the third set and Krajicek had just hit his 23rd ace when, despite blue sky all around, one grimly black cloud delivered its contents over Wimbledon and the covers had to come on again. As that was happening, however, one of the team, Mark Hillaby, 27, tripped, suffering a blow to the back of his head and neck. He was taken off on a stretcher but after a check-up in hospital was released and indeed was back on duty the next day. On the other hand the extra rain which fell while he was being carefully treated meant the court had become too wet for any more play, even though they were then back in action on Court One, where Goran Ivanisevic was in even more trouble than Sampras.

Stoltenberg is not one of the heaviest hitters in the game but he more than compensates in thought and accuracy and, despite double-faulting on the first point, he soon took the initiative by immediately breaking the Croatian. That was enough to settle the opening set, especially after Stoltenberg had retrieved a seventh game break-point created by a double fault with an ace.

In the second set, during which there was only one break point apiece, he stayed with the fourth seed to the tie-break, when Ivanisevic double-faulted to 0–4 and lost it 7–3. In the third set Ivanisevic broke for 4–3 but promptly surrendered his own serve again one game later and he only escaped a match point with a brave, deep second serve supported by a cross-court volley. So this set also went to a tie-break, where this time it was Stoltenberg who was undermined by an early double fault and he lost it 7–3.

With the clock showing 8.30 p.m., the light was fading quickly and they came off court. It meant that not one match in any event had been completed that day and with some already held over, Alan Mills, the referee, and his colleagues had to cope with 28 unfinished matches spread over 18 courts and a weather forecast that was not encouraging. A third Monday was beckoning.

Jason Stoltenberg played the match of his life to reach his first Grand Slam tournament semi-final.

WIMBLEDON

day **10**

THURSDAY 4 JULY

The pose of a well-beaten player as she looks across to see the winning smile on the face of her opponent.

'The thing with this Wimbledon climb is that I just went by match by match so I didn't realise I was going up such a big mountain until I got there. Then it got very steep. There was a little oxygen deprivation.'

Meredith McGrath, the Swiss-based American who loves climbing as a hobby, after losing to Arantxa Sanchez Vicario in her first Grand Slam semi-final.

And then there was one! At the end of Day Ten, another frustratingly disrupted three times by the weather, Todd Martin stood alone as the sole survivor of the 16 seeds when the quarter-finals of the men's singles were completed 24 hours late. Only once before had three unseeded competitors reached the semi-finals and that was in 1967 when there were only eight seeds. The defeat of three-times defending champion Pete Sampras and former runner-up Goran Ivanisevic, both by unseeded opponents, Richard Krajicek and Jason Stoltenberg, continuing the extraordinary run of upsets, round by round, brought this about.

Not only that but on a day when Martin closed the book on Britain's finest effort in men's singles for 23 years by Tim Henman, darkness fell with Steffi Graf, the defending champion chasing her seventh title in the ladies' singles, in all sorts of semi-final trouble against her deceptively dangerous, ever-resilient Japanese challenger, Kimiko Date.

Even with an 11 a.m. start on Centre Court to try and catch up some of the lost time and still give ladies' semi-finals day its due attention, renewed showers undermined the best intentions, adding to the hours the four players had to while away before their matches began.

Arantxa Sanchez Vicario was far from perturbed. When it was finally time for her to take to a now sunny stage, she annihilated the unseeded American, Meredith McGrath, 6–2, 6–1 in one minute over an hour. The Spaniard usually looks as if she is in a hurry and the scurrying was as impressive and effective as ever as she raced into a set and 2–1 lead. Then McGrath, a naturally athletic competitor with successes on grass in Birmingham (1996) and Eastbourne (1994) on her curriculum vitae, had even more trouble when she tweaked a muscle in the right leg which was already comprehensively bandaged.

She was allowed a three-minute injury delay, during which she lay on a towel on the court with her leg raised, but she was not exactly leaping about the

Visions of Wimbledon, on and off the courts, on a day of sunshine and showers. Opposite: Raindrops fall from the left arm of the much photographed Fred Perry statue.

Out for the count. Pete Sampras held out for just another 22 minutes before losing his match, unfinished overnight, against Richard Krajicek.

place on the restart. Nor, understandably, were there gestures of sympathy from the other side of the court. Sanchez was like a matador going for the kill. Even so McGrath, ranked 27, tried to play down the impact of her disability. 'Arantxa was hitting the ball so deep and basically passing me at will so I don't know, even if I had been 100 per cent healthy, I'd have done the job.'

Graf and Date arrived for the second semi-final when it was becoming touch and go whether there would be a reasonable amount of time for them to finish. In April, in the Fed Cup, Date had beaten Graf 12–10 in the third in Tokyo. It was the victory of her dreams and, by all accounts, she had not stopped reliving it. On grass, though, even she had suggested her task would be much harder and it certainly looked that way when Graf, full of bounce, was 4–0 up within 11 minutes.

Yet Date, whose game can look so predictable and ordinary, has that skil-

MaliVai Washington's extra experience finally ended a memorable Wimbledon for Alex Radulescu (bottom).

Graf was leading 6–2, 2–0 when things started to change. The polite little Japanese player began using her reliable groundstrokes to create the opportunities for her to send forehands winging their way down the German's unguarded backhand side or to take two or three gentle strides in to place volleys crisply and with perfect accuracy. The favourite had one chance to stem the onslaught with a point for 3–2 but instead Date broke her again and went on to level the match with six consecutive games by 8.57 p.m. when bad light meant another overnight delay. Not surprisingly, Date would have been happy to continue. A player who has just taken a set in that way always is.

While on any other day the defeats of Sampras and Ivanisevic, whom most had expected to clash in the semi-finals, would have been enormous shocks, that was hardly so on this occasion for both were ominously close to the precipice when they went home the night before.

Exactly four years to the day after he had won the first of his three consecutive titles, the American was unable to tame the pounding which 6ft 5in Krajicek had been starting to give him the previous evening. However much Sampras must have been hoping for a spectacular American Independence Day recovery on a new day, it was never more than a dream.

With Krajicek continuing to deliver aces and other winners, especially backhand passes, with enviable venom and admirable variety, the final chapter, which ended Sampras's run of 25 consecutive victories at The Championships, took just 22 minutes. 'I've won a lot of close matches on that court so this is a tough one to swallow,' said the world champion as the despair of his 7–5, 7–6, 6–4 defeat, not made easier by the thought of those chances he had to win the first two sets, sank in. 'I ran into a player who was very hot both yesterday and today and when that happens on grass you just have to accept it.'

ful ability to keep making returns down the middle, denying opponents the angles and openings they are trying to create and dragging them into baseline battles they certainly want to avoid. It had been the same in her two previous matches when she had patiently recovered from losing first sets to beat former champion Conchita Martinez, seeded three, and then Mary Pierce, seeded 13. Now Graf was being given the same tormenting treatment.

Tim Henman bids farewell to a legion of Centre Court supporters after 'the greatest tournament of my career so far' came to an end when he was beaten in the quarter-finals by Todd Martin (below).

As so often, the seventh game of what was to be the final set proved critical. Sampras, whose tennis throughout the year had somehow lacked the extra spark and penetration of a year earlier, double-faulted to 30–30. Then Krajicek, albeit on the first of them with a little help from the net, passed him with two more of those stunning, whipped backhands which had been so much a feature of his performance. A few minutes later, courtesy of his 29th ace, Krajicek rounded off his triumph with another service winner. However much others were surprised, he was not. 'I knew Pete was nervous. We were 2–2 in previous matches and I felt confident, with all the pressure on him, that I could beat him again.'

Ivanisevic put much of the blame for his 6–3, 7–6, 6–7, 7–6 defeat down to his playing 'two bad tie-breaks'. That was certainly so. He made a disastrous start in both and lost both 7–3. Having earned a reprieve overnight by saving that match point at 4–5 and taking the third-set tie-break 7–3, Ivanisevic was also hoping that it would be a new game on a new day. It could have been but, as the fourth seed acknowledged, he 'didn't make anything like enough passing shots and also wanted to hit too many winners, too quickly'. He had four break points in the remaining set but also had to save two break points to hold for 6–5 before it all went hopelessly wrong for him again in the tie-break when he lost the first six points.

For Stoltenberg, who had never gone beyond the third round before, it was a worthy reward for a match in which his temperament and tactics turned the key on the majority of the big points. And that makes the difference so often between winning and losing. It was much the same as MaliVai Washington beat the least likely of all the quarter-finalists, Alexander Radulescu. Washington saved two match points in the fourth set of a serve-dominated match in which the Romanian-born German hit another 32 aces to take his total for the tournament to

133 and did not have his serve broken until facing match point for the first time.

Meanwhile 'Henmania' as the tabloids had dubbed Tim Henman's success – twice the shop sold out of his pin badges and Nike, his clothing company, also had to send urgently for extra supplies – calmed down when, in a quarter-final four times interrupted by rain, he was beaten 7–6, 7–6, 6–4 by Todd Martin. The British number one was given a standing ovation as he left the Centre Court for, although disappointed, like the player himself, that he had been unable to grab two break points and three set points in the first set which might have made a difference, the crowd realised that Britain at last had another player with genuine world-class potential.

Curiously enough it was on those crisis points against him in the first set, four of which he saved with unreturnable serves, that Martin seemed to produce his best tennis. Beforehand, the consensus was that if both players performed to the peak of their proved ability so far, Martin, a former Australian Open finalist, would be favourite to win. In the event Martin did not play to his best but nor was Henman quite able to assert himself in the way he knew was necessary. Just occasionally, too, Henman's relative lack of experience played a part. In the tie-break which decided the important first set, Henman fought back from 1–4 to make it 5–5 with a flashing pass, only for Martin to reach set point with an ace, at which stage Henman double-faulted. 'It was probably a serve I shouldn't have hit,' he said. As he tossed the ball up for the second-serve delivery 'it was blowing around quite a lot in the wind. But I hit it . . . and missed it. It was as simple as that.'

On the other hand he could reflect on 'ten days which have made this the greatest tournament of my career so far and I hope I have many more, even better Wimbledons to come in the future. I've shown I can compete with some of the very top players. Now it's my job, my aim, to join them.'

For the third day in the second week, the weather did its worst. Although, thanks to another early start (11 a.m. on all courts), 40 matches were completed, including the safe passage by Steffi Graf through to the following day's ladies' singles final, many more were not. Most important among them were the two semi-finals of the men's singles.

Not a ball was struck on Centre Court after 3.07 p.m. and elsewhere, because of another of those freak situations where it was clearly raining on the main stage but not on No. 1 Court, 25 yards away, the last points of the day were played at 3.20 p.m. The players, officials and most of the spectators waited patiently, with Centre Court entertainment being provided – this time the crowd could watch and listen to Sir Peter Ustinov being interviewed – until 7.35 p.m., when Christopher Gorringe, Chief Executive of the All England Club, who this year was having to convey more bad news than good, announced play had been abandoned.

Todd Martin, the only surviving seed among those originally placed in the draw, and fellow American MaliVai Washington, who had just reached two sets all when the rain drove them off for a second and final time in the day, were scheduled to return at 11 a.m. the following day. Disappointing though it must have been to them, Richard Krajicek and Jason Stoltenberg, who had not got on court at all, would also start at 11 a.m. but on No. 1 Court. There were two good reasons for that – and precedents for it. One was to make sure their match was resolved in plenty of time for the winner to think about and prepare for the final the next day; however, it was also hoped that the renewed showers still being forecast would stay away at least long enough for the ladies' singles final to go ahead on Centre Court at 2 p.m.

Looking ahead to her 36th clash with Arantxa Sanchez Vicario, the last 16 of them in finals, including Wimbledon 1995, Graf, who had taken just 26 minutes to win the third set delayed overnight

for a 6–2, 2–6, 6–3 defeat of Kimiko Date, said, 'I hope people aren't getting bored by us playing in so many finals.'

As for the final stages of her match with Date, Graf, who had certainly looked in trouble the night before when from 6–2, 2–0 she lost six consecutive games, began with an ace and never again looked in more than token danger. She looked and sounded awful but assured everyone that the severe head cold which had prevented her from practising for three days was now running away and that she felt 'great'. Her serving was certainly much more positive than the night before and the forehand starting to be back in the groove, while she relished the two heavily spun inside-out backhand returns which helped her make the break she wanted for 4–2.

Although Date, with her unorthodox but impressively effective forehand, kept fighting by saving two match points in the eighth game, her spark the night before had vanished. A tame backhand gave Graf a third match point and then a forehand error confirmed Graf's place in her eighth Wimbledon singles final.

Perhaps it had something to do with the significance of the occasion or

With play halted by so much rain, Allsport's Stu Forster found time to photograph some off-court activities in black and white. Below: Through the ivy-clad façade towards the outside courts. Bottom left: Making plates bearing players' names for the scoreboards. Bottom right: Spectators bustling to and fro.

Above: The inevitable Mexican wave.

Left: The official cushion stall.

Right: Propped together, a young couple grab some sleep.

WIMBLEDON CUSHIONS £5.00

maybe it was just because they knew each other's game so well, but the fluctuating quality of the tennis by both players in the four sets Martin and Washington were able to play meant it was hardly gripping entertainment. In keeping with their established personalities, the tennis was more safe and steadfast than adventurous.

Washington, aiming to become the first black player since the late Arthur Ashe, the legendary champion in 1975, to reach the final, was increasingly winning the hitherto neutral crowd to his side by the end of the fourth set because of the way he had twice fought back from being a set down. He, like the spectators, had sensed that Martin, who towers over most people, was again making a surprising number of tentative volleys, often after having played perfectly to create the point-winning position.

Martin, who broke Washington's opening service game, led 5–3, was then broken himself when he failed to convert an admittedly difficult mid-court volley off a sharp service return but still took the set with the help of his opponent's errors in the 12th game. Washington, despite needing pain-killing tablets from trainer Bill Norris – he was suffering from an already existing injury and so could not receive on-court physical treatment – stepped up the pressure to break for 3–2 in the second set with three sparkling returns followed by Martin's double fault on break point.

The third set went like the first, with Martin breaking for 2–0 but being broken back to 5–4 and so they moved on to a tie-break, in which Washington led 3–1, trailed 3–6 and was eventually beaten 6–8. At last during the fourth set one could sense the crowd's enthusiasm stirring, especially as Washington once more demonstrated not just his resilience but also the confidence to produce a wider range of winners. From his point of view, when they had to take cover and pray for better weather the next morning, the score was 5–7, 6–4, 6–7, 6–3. It was anyone's guess about what would occur next, both in terms of the tennis – and the weather.

As for the men's doubles, where the finalists should also by then have been known, Byron Black and Grant Connell, a new Zimbabwe–Canada combination this year, had booked their place with a straight-sets win over Ellis Ferreira from South Africa and Holland's Jan Siemerink, but Todd Woodbridge and Mark Woodforde, the defending champions, were still one game away, at 6–3, 7–6, 6–5, from beating fellow Australians Pat Rafter and Mark Philippoussis in a sometimes tense affair in which the rivalries were clearly defined.

In the ladies' doubles, Sanchez and Jana Novotna continued the defence of their title with a 6–3, 6–3 defeat of Holland's Kristie Boogert and Irina Spirlea from Romania but that was only to reach the quarter-finals. And Sanchez still had other, more important matters on her mind. Meanwhile Liz Smylie, a former champion, and Linda Wild went sailing through to the semi-finals in the Sanchez–Novotna half of the draw, when Mary Joe Fernandez, partnering Lindsay Davenport, had to quit with more back trouble at 3–5 in the first set.

Match of the day in the mixed doubles was on Court Three where Martina Navratilova produced the crafty lob which ultimately set up the chance for her also to make the forehand volley which clinched her progress into the quarter-finals with Jonathan Stark 7–6, 6–7, 7–5 against Marcos Ondruska and Karen Kschwendt. When the Americans were leading 4–1 in the second set, some of the crowd in the back row of the stand assumed Navratilova was safe and for a while turned their backs on her to watch a golden oldies doubles next door on No. 2 Court.

Here Ilie Nastase, still the joker, who never misses a trick to provoke a laugh, usually at the expense of others rather than himself, had Tom Okker as his straight man against those wily Australians, John Newcombe and Tony Roche. Nastase and Okker won 7–6, 4–6,

6–3 but only after Nastase had told Okker, who was known at his peak as 'The Flying Dutchman', 'you're not that any more, you're the Dying Dutchman.' And that was before Okker double-faulted twice when he was serving for the match at 5–1 in the third. 'I'll give your racket to my son,' he said before looking towards nine-year-old Nick sitting in the front row and saying, 'C'mon, son, come and show Mr Okker how to serve a second serve!' The lad sensibly declined. The crowd enjoyed the tomfoolery . . . and then turned their attention again to Navratilova.

Some had also been hoping to see Britain's Martin Lee bid for a place in the semi-finals of the boys' singles but the rain put a stop to that and also to a first match for Lee and David Sherwood (replacing the injured James Trotman, who won the title with Lee 12 months earlier) in the boys' doubles. It was just as well this event had been reduced from 32 pairs to 16 this year.

MaliVai Washington twice fought back to be two sets all in his semi-final against Todd Martin before yet again the rain returned.

With the men's singles semi-finals safely completed in good time – and amid much drama as MaliVai Washington spectacularly recovered from 1–5 in the final set against Todd Martin to create what was billed internationally as Wimbledon's first all-unseeded final against Richard Krajicek, as the Dutchman was not originally seeded – Steffi Graf and Arantxa Sanchez Vicario presented themselves in customary style spot on 2 p.m. for the ladies' singles final.

At 2.04 p.m., however, when they had barely started their warm-up, they returned to the dressing rooms. The rain, which had already briefly delayed the start of the men's matches at 11 a.m., had begun again. Fortunately, though, it was the last shower of the day and by 2.57 p.m., when Graf began serving at the start of what for her quickly became a sunshine performance, there were blue skies to match.

Graf was to win 6–3, 7–5 and, apart from being her seventh success at Wimbledon, edging her ever closer at least to equalling Martina Navratilova's record of nine singles titles, it was surely fitting that it was on the stage where she finds the most inspiration that, at the same time, she won the 100th title of her career.

With Graf playing far better than she had done in the previous year's wonderful final and the Spaniard, who lost that one 8–6 in the third, providing a less feisty challenge this time, it was not one of the most memorable among their clashes. Yet it was one Graf clearly relished more than most. 'Simply unbelievable. It's just like a dream,' she said at the end of an afternoon in which, once her forehand found its groove, it hardly wavered.

Not only that but, as Graf confided later, she could so easily once again have been beaten by health problems. Whatever doubts any sceptics may have had about the seriousness of the knee injury which prevented her from practising on grass until 48 hours before the tournament began, no one who had listened to her coughing and blowing her nose, or saw her after her narrow squeak against Kimiko Date in the semi-finals,

Same day, same place, same faces, same result. As in the 1995 final, Steffi Graf's all-round skills, more pronounced than ever, it seemed, made sure she kept the trophy against Arantxa Sanchez Vicario.

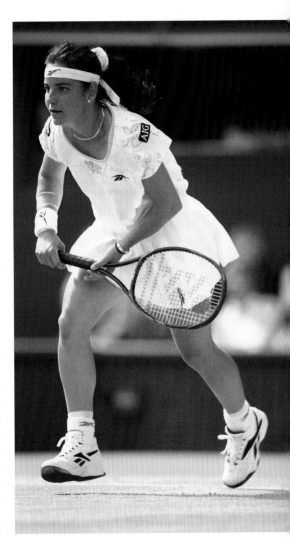

could seriously have suggested the problems were not genuine. On the eve of the final Graf still had a temperature and, had she followed medical advice, would probably have stayed in bed. But that is not Steffi Graf and particularly not Steffi Graf at Wimbledon.

Sanchez, who won the toss, made Graf serve in the opening game and the ploy could have worked, for Graf twice faced break points, the second after a fluke forehand, lifted return, but the Spaniard was just long with an ambitious lob and in essence never had more than a flickering chance. After some cut-and-thrust exchanges in the opening games, the German surged ahead when she broke for 3–1 and in next to no time had taken the set and reached 4–1 in the second, with a prime mixture of strong serves and even stronger forehands. Yet, for no obvious reason, after hitting an ace to reach 40–15 in the sixth game, she nearly lost her grip.

The Spaniard dashed round the court to hit scorching returns, some teasing lobs and even one or two trenchant volleys and then broke back in the most extraordinary fashion. Graf, who looked perfectly placed to put away an overhead, missed it completely. Although she was able to swing round and make a second attempt off the bounce, Sanchez was there to pounce and put away a forehand. 'She wanted to hit the overhead too hard,' said the challenger. 'I can't remember ever doing that before. It was a little embarrassing,' said Graf with a grin.

Sanchez was in this rousing, swashbuckling mood for the next few games, breaking back again to 5–5 when Graf first served for the title but then a fall on the first point of the 11th game provided the chance for the German's forehand to resume as the decisive factor. Serving for victory a second time, Graf made no mistake and in doing so won the 20th Grand Slam singles title of her career. Only Margaret Court, with 24, remained ahead of her. But for how long? Graf, who hugged the trophy to her closer than ever on her lap of honour after the presentation ceremony, said: 'You want to hold on to the moment but the moment goes so quickly. There was a lot of joy inside me.

'Having missed out so much on practice, I just felt physically I wouldn't get through it all the way. But the last three years I've had these decisions, to play or not to play, and I've always chosen to play and take the risk. Every time it's worked well.'

For Sanchez there was still doubles to come but it was also time for the Centre Court to reflect on the way MaliVai Washington had almost miraculously clawed his way back from 1–5 in that final set of his semi-final against Todd Martin to become the first black finalist since Arthur Ashe, his boyhood hero, became champion by out-psyching Jimmy Connors, the defending champion, 21 years earlier.

'I was only six at the time but I remember seeing the match point of the final on television,' said Washington. 'It's an honour to be the first since Arthur. I just hope I can play well enough in the final to encourage more black kids into tennis.'

Washington's equable temperament, despite one outburst, for which he later apologised, was just as significant as his tennis. His despair with the line calling came when umpire Bruno Rebeuh ordered a point to be replayed after a ridiculously prolonged discussion with his service linesman over whether a serve which looked well out and would have given him three break points at 6–6 was, or was not, within the range of cyclops. Despite the distraction he soon shrugged it aside and continued to take full advantage of a good draw and the shortcomings of others to reach the final.

While he made few unforced errors, Martin, by his own admission, 'froze up' when leading 5–1 in the final set. 'I regret getting tight but I couldn't control it.' There were three double faults when Martin first served for the match and two more when he tried a second time. And after another rain delay when Martin was leading 7–6, Washington came back out and served a love game to underline his resilience. It gave him the

'No, no, it's my turn this year,' Sanchez jokes as she fleetingly hugs the trophy she hopes will one day be hers.

A couple of hours earlier on the same court, Todd Martin could only reflect sadly on letting slip a 5-1 final-set lead against MaliVai Washington.

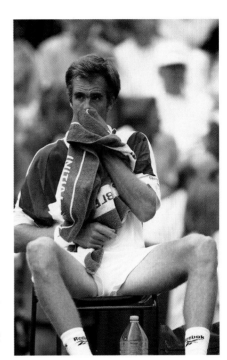

Todd Martin's reflections on the loss of a 5–1 lead in the final set of his men's singles semi-final. 'You get mad at yourself, you laugh at yourself. You experience the whole gamut of emotions. I've never felt a feeling like today. I know if I had won it would have been the greatest feeling I've had in the game. Everybody feels tight at some time. You try to go through the rituals. Focus on breathing. Make sure you're moving your feet. When your muscles get tight it's probably because of a lack of oxygen. I must not have been sucking in enough and blowing out enough.'

Jason Stoltenberg (previous pages) was overpowered by Richard Krajicek, whom he congratulates (below) on becoming the first Dutch player to reach the men's singles final.

Another familiar sight (opposite), as Australians Todd Woodbridge (left) and Mark Woodforde celebrate winning the men's doubles title for a fourth consecutive year, the first pair to do so this century. Overleaf: They are on the far side of the court in this net exchange with Grant Connell (left) and Byron Black.

momentum to produce more and more superb returns against a still nervous and erratic opponent until he broke for 9–8 after another Martin double fault and a netted low forehand. Washington was 0–30 serving for the match but took the next four points, completing his 5–7, 6–4, 6–7, 6–3, 10–8 victory in three hours 49 minutes of playing time with a determined forehand cross-court volley.

All Martin could do was try to put a brave face on the sort of collapse which must have made Jana Novotna feel better. Meanwhile, on No. 1 Court, Richard Krajicek was taking little more than an hour and a half to overpower Australian Jason Stoltenberg 7–5, 6–2, 6–1 with 15 aces and an increasingly blistering heavy artillery of groundstokes. Stoltenberg, who had exceeded his and every other Australian's wildest dreams in reaching the last four, gallantly stayed with his bigger, stronger and more capable opponent as long as he could but long before the end knew it was a formality.

Once Larisa Neiland and Meredith McGrath beat three-times former champions Gigi Fernandez and Natasha Zvereva 6–4, 3–6, 11–9 to reach the final of the ladies' doubles, it became inevitable that some matches would have

to be carried over until a third Monday for the Latvian at that stage still faced the possibility of four matches with Mark Woodforde in the mixed doubles. Meanwhile Woodforde and Todd Woodbridge, after dropping the first set, were making history on Centre Court as they took supreme charge for a 4–6, 6–1, 6–3, 6–2 defeat of Byron Black and Grant Connell, from Zimbabwe and Canada respectively, to become the first pair since 1901 to win the men's doubles title for four consecutive years.

Hopes of further British success in the juniors, after the 1995 triumph by Martin Lee and James Trotman, were sustained when, although Lee was beaten in the quarter-final of the singles, 7–5, 6–4 by Ivan Ljubicic of Croatia, both he with David Sherwood, who was deputising for the injured Trotman, and Ben Haran with Simon Pender reached the semi-finals of the doubles. And to keep hopes high, there was one British success when Jo Durie, partnered by American Anne Smith, won the 35 and over invitation doubles 6–3, 6–2 against Yvonne Vermaak of South Africa and Mima Jausovec, formerly of Yugoslavia but now of Slovakia.

It had been a long, long day. And another was in store.

Richard Krajicek (previous pages) kisses the most coveted trophy in lawn tennis after his ruthlessly powerful consistency was too much for MaliVai Washington (opposite).

Gone are the days when players had to talk nicely to BBC Television to see if they would let them have a copy of any of their matches which had been recorded on Centre Court or No. 1 Court. The All England Club now presents all players involved in singles matches on these courts with a videotape of the game as a gift.

When the fortnight began, bookmakers William Hill were offering 1,000–1 against a men's singles final between Richard Krajicek and MaliVai Washington. They were also quoting Krajicek at 40–1 for the title and Washington at 150–1. On the day of the final it was rather different. Krajicek was 1–4 favourite with Washington 11–4.

At last Richard Krajicek became famous for something more than having described the majority of women players as 'lazy fat pigs'. At 6.07 on what at last was a settled summer evening, the powerfully built, 6ft 5in Dutchman dropped to his knees and, as Paul Hayward of *The Daily Telegraph* wrote, was 'like a pig in muck' as he rolled back on Centre Court in ecstatic disbelief after producing a display of magnificently controlled, all-round aggression to become Wimbledon champion.

Thanks to further rain delays, exactly four hours had elapsed since he struck the first of countless penetrating serves when he wound up for the last of his equally significant huge forehands to beat MaliVai Washington 6–3, 6–4, 6–3. The actual playing time had been one hour 33 minutes and, bravely though Washington fought to find a way into the match, in reality he never quite succeeded. Indeed, he acknowledged that later when he said, 'I kept looking for a little window to go through but all credit to Rich. He kept the window locked.'

It had been a quite brilliant performance by Krajicek, who took masterly control of the match with a stunning start and then, after the last and longest (at 67 minutes) of the three delays, even managed to step up his game. 'For a split second at the end I asked myself, "Is the match really over or am I making a fool of myself?" But I didn't hear anyone laughing so I knew it was true,' said the Czech-born Dutchman.

Though he dropped his serve for the only time in the match in the sixth game of the third set, it followed a spurt of 14 consecutive points which, had he not realised already, told Washington that his chances of winning were fast disappearing. In retrospect Krajicek, who was high enough (14) in the rankings when the seeds were announced, should have been included. First-round defeats, once when he *was* seeded, in the two previous years probably swung the decision against him. Then when Thomas Muster, who was supposed to be the seventh seed, withdrew injured after the draw had

taken place, Krajicek, as the next-highest ranked unseeded player, was moved by the Committee to the Austrian's position in the draw (and his spot filled by Anders Jarryd as a lucky loser).

'I don't think I've proved anything to the Committee by winning without being seeded, but I think next year I'll get a seed,' said the new champion with a knowing smile. In the view of the All England Club, however, Krajicek had been seeded all along. At The Champions' Dinner that night, the Club Chairman, John Curry, assured Krajicek that he had been seeded, quoting the *Oxford English Dictionary*'s definition of a seeded player as one who had been placed in the draw – which was certainly so in his case. Curiously enough his original place in the draw would have meant his taking on Pete Sampras, the defending champion, one round earlier than he did. On his form throughout the fortnight, the outcome would probably have been just the same.

John McEnroe was just one of those eager to congratulate Krajicek on a success he was convinced would happen one day. Tactically, technically and thoughtfully, he had handsomely confirmed that view. The win made him Holland's first winner of any Grand Slam singles title, earned him £392,500 and also restored him to the world's top ten for the first time since 1993. Yet far more than that, he and Washington had shown that you do not always need the top names or the most flamboyant personalities to produce tennis worthy of this occasion. Most of the points were decided by winners and there were more rallies in the three sets than in the Sampras–Becker and Sampras–Ivanisevic finals in the two previous years put together.

Stanley Franker, Holland's Davis Cup captain, had spoken earlier of how there had been so many times when Krajicek had taken an extra opponent on to the court – 'himself'. Increasingly during the second week of Wimbledon '96, after losing just one set to Brett Steven, that was no longer so. There was an almost

The All England
Lawn Tennis & Croquet Club Wimbledon

Church Road Wimbledon
London SW19 5AE
Telephone 0181-944 1066
Fax 0181-947 8752

Press Information

STATEMENT FROM CLUB SPOKESPERSON
REGARDING THE STREAKER ON CENTRE COURT

We have never had a streaker on Centre Court before, so I suppose it was inevitable
eventually. Whilst we do not wish to condone the practice, it did at least provide some
light amusement for our loyal and patient supporters, who have had a trying time
during the recent bad weather.

ENDS

For further information please contact:

Johnny Perkins / Philippa Haslegrave
Lowe Bell Good Relations
0181 971 2529

OR

Press Bureau, Scotland Yard
Tel: 0171 230 2171

*This year there was an extra diversion just before the start of the men's
singles final, when an unscheduled extra 'performer' amused the
crowd and focused the attention of both amateur and professional
photographers. The statement later from the All England Club said
all that needed to be said.*

*Opposite: The true centre of attention. Richard Krajicek falls to the
ground in joyous disbelief at his success.*

The battle is over and MaliVai Washington accepts that his opponent was a worthy champion.

arrogant and brutal confidence in the way he opened up the court to put away backhands in particular with such command. If, as he insisted, there had been butterflies beforehand, the entrance of a streaker just when they were posing for photographers at the net before beginning the warm-up drove them away.

Having demonstrated straightaway that his serve, which produced another 14 aces on the day for a tournament total of 147, was in such good working order, he was equally convincing with his returns as he promptly took Washington's opening service game, which was also enough for the set. It took him 33 minutes and he dropped only three points in his five service games.

Raindrops were already falling on the heads before Washington started the second set in a revitalised vein which suggested that he at least felt he could repeat his effort in twice coming from behind to win in his two previous matches. It was a vain hope. After the first delay at 1–1 there was only time for Washington to produce the winning volley which made it 2–1 and for Krajicek to reach 30–30 on serve in the next game before they were driven off again, this time for 47 minutes. There was no way Krajicek was going to lose concentration, however. A series of fine returns brought about the break which allowed him to serve out the second set in the tenth game. And after a rain delay of 67 minutes at the end of the opening game of the third set, he resumed just as emphatically and broke for 2–1 after drawing in his opponent only to leave him stranded by a rasping forehand pass.

In the final game there were two more of those wonderfully timed, perfectly weighted, dipping returns which made Krajicek such a formidable champion and although his legs slipped from under him as he made his service return on the first match point, on the second he patiently probed Washington's defences before making the cobra-like forehand strike.

Washington, who won so many new friends with his performances through-

out the fortnight and more later when despite obvious disappointment he joined in the salute to Krajicek and Steffi Graf at The Champions' Dinner, said the whole Wimbledon experience for him was 'difficult to put into words. It's what you dream about. And my dream almost came true.'

Meanwhile the scramble was on to try and complete as many events as possible on time and in all but the ladies' doubles, the mixed doubles and the junior girls' doubles it was successful, though not without some more painful departures. Martina Navratilova's hopes of drawing level with Billie Jean King's record of 20 Wimbledon titles were thwarted, possibly for ever, when she and Jonathan Stark, winners in 1995, were beaten 7–6, 7–6 in the quarter-finals of the mixed doubles by Grant Connell and Lindsay Davenport. As she walked off No. 1 Court for the last time, Navratilova turned round to look at the four stands soon to be demolished and then knelt down to take a few strands of the grass with her.

Just before Krajicek began his own demolition job on Washington, the final British junior hopes also went tumbling down as Ben Haran and Simon Pender were overpowered physically more than anything in losing 6–3, 6–4 to the triumphant Italian–Canadian combination of Daniele Bracciali and Jocelyn Robichaud, who then returned to court to add the Wimbledon title to success at the Australian Open over Lee and Trotman. In the final they were also too strong, 6–2, 6–4, for South Africans Damien Roberts and Wesley Whitehouse, who had just edged out Britain's Martin Lee and David Sherwood in two tie-breaks.

The men's 35 and over invitation doubles final was won by Wojtek Fibak of Poland and the American, Tim Wilkison, who beat Pavel Slozil and Tomas Smid, those stalwarts from the Czech Republic, 6–2, 5–7, 6–1, while in a nostalgic final to the 45 and over men's invitation doubles, which was also the final match during The Championships to take place on No. 1 Court, Australians

Spectators queue for the chance to watch matches at Wimbledon free of charge as the play runs into Monday.

and Helena Sukova, who had already beaten the defending champions, Arantxa Sanchez Vicario and Jana Novotna, late the previous night and then Liz Smylie and Linda Wild that morning, were leading Meredith McGrath and Larisa Neiland 5–7, 7–5, 4–1, and on the morning of the tournament's third Monday, when it took them all of five minutes to round off that third set 6–1, she was still, at 15 years and 282 days, three days younger than Lottie Dod had been when she won the ladies' singles in 1887.

Lottie Dod took the court in her day in a long white skirt which showed 'just a glimpse of stout black woollen stockings and just as stout black shoes'. Where other competitors favoured boaters, Dod had her hair tucked under a white flannel cap as she defeated Blanche Bingley 6–2, 6–0. Hingis, with modern skirt and top and the almost constant smile of someone who genuinely enjoys playing tennis, was modest about her achievement, quick to remind everyone that it was only the doubles, not the singles, but added that to win any title at Wimbledon was 'out of this world'. One hopes she will for ever have such enthusiasm.

Meanwhile, with the gates thrown open and the admission free, a crowd of 13,518, some because it offered a once-in-a-lifetime opportunity to see inside the gates but most of them genuine tennis fans, flocked in for the eight matches which remained to be played, all but two of them in the mixed doubles.

It was 11 a.m. when Christopher Gorringe, Chief Executive of the All England Club, welcomed everyone to the 14th 'and hopefully the final day of the Wimbledon fortnight' but it was another 15 minutes before play began to allow latecomers to take their seats.

It was the atmosphere of the famous Middle Sunday all over again and it ended, as it began, with triumph for Sukova. She and her brother Cyril Suk, both of whom had won the title before with other partners, beat Neiland and Mark Woodforde 6–3, 3–6, 6–2 in the final.

John Alexander and Phil Dent beat Marty Riessen and Sherwood Stewart from the United States 7–6, 6–2.

Nearly three hours after the first all-unseeded men's final, more history was close to being made on the Centre Court. When play was suspended because of yet another shower at 8.56 p.m., Martina Hingis was two games away from becoming the youngest champion in one of the five principal events. She

Suk and Sukova were clearly moved to win as a team. Cyril, who according to his sister had turned green at the end, had been thinking of his late mother, Vera, and the singles final she had played on that same court in 1962. Helena had played four hours 23 minutes that day completing the ladies' doubles and then the quarter-finals, semi-finals and final of the mixed. Neiland, with the same schedule, had played even longer, four hours 46 minutes, to finish runner-up in both events.

'I can't really take it in,' said Sukova. 'It's not just the sets I've played but the tension was there all the time.' It was a final unscheduled day of fine tennis and glorious enjoyment for all concerned, complete with Mexican waves, wolf whistles and a single bouquet of flowers thrown on to the court at the end of the ladies' doubles, clearly intended for Hingis. It was a fitting farewell to Wimbledon '96.

Below: Helena Sukova (left) was thrilled to have played her part in helping Martina Hingis become the youngest winner of any of the five principal titles in the history of The Championships when they won the ladies' doubles.

Overleaf: The packed Centre Court relishing the thrilling atmosphere and captivating, history-making tennis on the extra day needed to bring down the curtain on Wimbledon '96.

The Ladies' Doubles Championship
Helena Sukova and Martina Hingis

The Ladies' Singles Championship
Steffi Graf

The Mixed Doubles Championship
Helena Sukova and Cyril Suk

The 35 and over Gentlemen's Invitation Doubles
Wojtek Fibak and Tim Wilkison
(Trophy accepted by Tim Wilkison)

The 35 and over Ladies' Invitation Doubles
Anne Smith and Jo Durie

The 45 and over Gentlemen's Invitation Doubles
John Alexander and Phil Dent

The Gentlemen's Singles Championship
Richard Krajicek

The Gentlemen's Doubles Championship
Todd Woodbridge and Mark Woodforde

The Boys' Doubles Championship
Jocelyn Robichaud and Daniele Bracciali

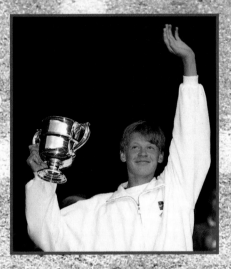

The Boys' Singles Championship
Vladimir Voltchkov

The Girls' Doubles Championship
Amelie Mauresmo and
Olga Barabanschikova

The Girls' Singles Championship
Amelie Mauresmo

Main photo: The impressive new No. 1 Court takes shape.

Inset: Head Groundsman Eddie Seaward on the turf already laid in readiness for the 1997 Championships.

CHAMPIONSHIP
RECORDS *1996*

LADIES

60 Adams Miss K.M. *(USA)*
88 Appelmans Miss S. *(Belgium)*
6 Arendt Miss N.J. *(USA)*
Barclay Miss C.G. *(Australia)*
28 Basuki Miss Y. *(Indonesia)*
3 Baudone Miss N. *(Italy)*
105 Begerow Miss P. *(Germany)*
83 Bobkova Miss R. *(Czech Republic)*
Bollegraf Miss M.M. *(Netherlands)*
42 Boogert Miss K. *(Netherlands)*
43 Bradtke Mrs N. *(Australia)*
109 Cacic Miss S. *(USA)*
58 Callens Miss E.S.H. *(Belgium)*
25 Carlsson Miss A. *(Sweden)*
Cecchini Miss A-M. *(Italy)*
40 Cocheteux Miss A. *(France)*
113 Coetzer Miss A.J. *(South Africa)*
29 Courtois Miss L. *(Belgium)*
46 Cristea Miss C. *(Romania)*
Crook Miss H. *(Great Britain)*
Dahlman Miss N. *(Finland)*
48 Date Miss K. *(Japan)*
64 Davenport Miss L.A. *(USA)*
Davies Miss V. *(Great Britain)*
De Lone Miss E.R. *(USA)*
23 de Swardt Miss M. *(South Africa)*
117 Dechaume-Balleret Mrs A. *(France)*
122 Dechy Miss N. *(France)*
Demongeot Miss I. *(France)*
Dhenin Miss C. *(France)*
10 Dopfer Miss S. *(Austria)*
27 Dragomir Miss R. *(Romania)*
124 Drake Miss M. *(Canada)*
100 Ellwood Miss A. *(Australia)*
115 Endo Miss M. *(Japan)*
34 Farina Miss S. *(Italy)*
118 Feber Miss N. *(Belgium)*
72 Fernandez Miss G. *(USA)*
112 Fernandez Miss M.J. *(USA)*
75 Frazier Miss A. *(USA)*
9 Fusai Miss A. *(France)*
Garrone Miss L. *(Italy)*
59 Gavaldon Miss A. *(Mexico)*
Ghirardi Miss L. *(France)*
30 Glass Miss A. *(Germany)*
101 Godridge Miss K. *(Australia)*
38 Golarsa Miss L. *(Italy)*
77 Gorrochategui Miss I. *(Argentina)*
1 Graf Miss S. *(Germany)*
Graham Miss D.A. *(USA)*
94 Grande Miss R. *(Italy)*
127 Grossman Miss A. *(USA)*
86 Grzybowska Miss M. *(Poland)*
44 Guse Miss K-A. *(Australia)*
65 Habsudova Miss K. *(Slovakia)*
Hetherington Miss J.M. *(Canada)*
16 Hingis Miss M. *(Switzerland)*
53 Hiraki Miss R. *(Japan)*
97 Huber Miss A. *(Germany)*
4 Husarova Miss J. *(Slovakia)*
24 Hy-Boulais Mrs P. *(Canada)*
71 Jecmenica Miss T. *(Yugoslavia)*
Jeyaseelan Miss S. *(Canada)*
Jones Miss D.J. *(Australia)*
121 Kamio Miss Y. *(Japan)*
19 Kamstra Miss P. *(Netherlands)*
111 Kandarr Miss J. *(Germany)*
92 Kijimuta Miss N.K. *(Japan)*
Koutstaal Miss M. *(Netherlands)*
Krajcovicova Miss D. *(Slovakia)*
103 Kremer Miss A. *(Luxemburg)*
Krizan Miss T. *(Slovenia)*
82 Kruger Miss J. *(South Africa)*
26 Kschwendt Miss K. *(Germany)*
107 Labat Miss F. *(Argentina)*
Lake Miss V. *(Great Britain)*
Langrova Miss P. *(Czech Republic)*
98 Leon Garcia Miss G. *(Spain)*
Lettiere Miss A. *(USA)*
57 Likhovtseva Miss E. *(Russia)*
Lindstrom Miss M. *(Sweden)*
22 Lubiani Miss F. *(Italy)*
Lugina Miss O. *(Ukraine)*
Lutrova Miss J. *(Russia)*
125 Makarova Miss E. *(Russia)*
17 Maleeva Miss M. *(Bulgaria)*
31 Martinek Miss V. *(Germany)*
33 Martinez Miss C. *(Spain)*
116 McGrath Miss M.J. *(USA)*
37 McNeil Miss L.M. *(USA)*
McQuillan Miss R. *(Australia)*
56 Medvedeva Miss N. *(Ukraine)*
Meier Miss S. *(Germany)*
Melicharova Miss E. *(Czech Republic)*
119 Miller Miss A. *(USA)*
14 Miller Miss M. *(Great Britain)*
87 Miyagi Miss N. *(Japan)*
Montalvo Miss L. *(Argentina)*
36 Montolio Miss A. *(Spain)*
55 Morariu Miss C. *(USA)*
Muric Miss M. *(Croatia)*
47 Nagatsuka Miss K. *(Japan)*
Nagelsen Miss B. *(USA)*
5 Nagyova Miss H. *(Slovakia)*
Navratilova Miss M. *(USA)*
61 Neiland Mrs L. *(Latvia)*
15 Nejedly Miss J. *(Canada)*
Nideffer Mrs R. *(South Africa)*
32 Novotna Miss J. *(Czech Republic)*
69 Nowak Miss K. *(Poland)*
85 Olsza Miss A. *(Poland)*
93 Oremans Miss M. *(Netherlands)*
Papadaki Miss C. *(Greece)*
74 Park Miss S-H. *(South Korea)*
68 Paz Miss M. *(Argentina)*
89 Perfetti Miss F. *(Italy)*
49 Pierce Miss M. *(France)*
Pitkowski Miss S. *(France)*
70 Pizzichini Miss G. *(Italy)*
Pleming Miss L. *(Australia)*
39 Po Miss K. *(USA)*
7 Porwik Miss C. *(Germany)*
Pratt Miss N.J. *(Australia)*
Price Miss T.A. *(South Africa)*
Probst Miss W. *(Germany)*
Pullin Miss J.M. *(Great Britain)*
Radford Miss K. *(Australia)*
76 Randriantefy Miss D. *(Madagascar)*
35 Raymond Miss L.M. *(USA)*
Reece Miss S. *(USA)*
2 Richterova Miss L. *(Czech Republic)*
62 Rinaldi-Stunkel Mrs K.S. *(USA)*
18 Rittner Miss B. *(Germany)*
41 Ruano Pascual Miss V. *(Spain)*
90 Sanchez Lorenzo Mrs M. *(Spain)*
96 Sanchez Vicario Miss A. *(Spain)*
91 Sawamatsu Miss N. *(Japan)*
106 Schett Miss B. *(Austria)*
Schneider Miss C. *(Germany)*
63 Schnell Miss M. *(Austria)*
50 Schnyder Miss P. *(Switzerland)*
81 Schultz-McCarthy Mrs B. *(Netherlands)*
128 Seles Miss M. *(USA)*
95 Serra-Zanetti Miss A. *(Italy)*
99 Shriver Miss P.H. *(USA)*
Siddall Miss S-A. *(Great Britain)*
45 Sidot Miss A-G. *(France)*
Simpson Miss R. *(Canada)*
54 Singer Miss C. *(Germany)*
78 Smashnova Miss A. *(Israel)*
79 Smith Miss S. *(Great Britain)*
Smylie Mrs P.D. *(Australia)*
80 Spirlea Miss I. *(Romania)*
Strandlund Miss M. *(Sweden)*
11 Stubbs Miss R.P. *(Australia)*
126 Studenikova Miss K. *(Slovakia)*
120 Suarez Miss P. *(Argentina)*
104 Sugiyama Miss A. *(Japan)*
102 Sukova Miss H. *(Czech Republic)*
Tanasugarn Miss T. *(Thailand)*
Tarabini Miss P. *(Argentina)*
20 Tauziat Miss N. *(France)*
52 Taylor Miss C. *(Great Britain)*
Temesvari Miss A. *(Hungary)*
110 Testud Miss S. *(France)*
123 Van Roost Mrs D. *(Belgium)*
Vildova Miss H. *(Czech Republic)*
13 Viollet Miss R. *(Great Britain)*
Vis Miss C.M. *(Netherlands)*
114 Wagner Mrs E. *(Germany)*
Wainwright Miss A.M.H. *(Great Britain)*
51 Ward Miss J. *(Great Britain)*
84 Watanabe Miss J. *(USA)*
67 Werdel Witmeyer Mrs M. *(USA)*
108 Whitlinger-Jones Mrs T.S. *(USA)*
66 Wiesner Mrs J.K. *(Austria)*
12 Wild Miss L.M. *(USA)*
8 Wood Miss C.J. *(Great Britain)*
Woodroffe Miss L.A. *(Great Britain)*
Yoshida Miss Y. *(Japan)*
73 Zrubakova Miss R. *(Slovakia)*
21 Zvereva Miss N. *(Belarus)*

GENTLEMEN

Adams D. *(South Africa)*
96 Agassi A. *(USA)*
7 Alami K. *(Morocco)*
Albano P. *(Argentina)*
89 Arazi H. *(Morocco)*
Ardinghi M. *(Italy)*
Arthurs W. *(Australia)*
Bale L.J. *(South Africa)*
Barnard M. *(South Africa)*
103 Bates M.J. *(Great Britain)*
128 Becker B. *(Germany)*
87 Beecher C. *(Great Britain)*
Behrens B. *(USA)*
Belloli J. *(USA)*
Bergh R. *(Sweden)*
69 Bjorkman J. *(Sweden)*
6 Black B. *(Zimbabwe)*
Black W. *(Zimbabwe)*
113 Boetsch A. *(France)*
35 Bouteyre P. *(France)*
Broad N. *(Great Britain)*
Bruno N. *(Italy)*
Cannon S. *(USA)*
124 Caratti C. *(Italy)*
126 Carbonell T. *(Spain)*
71 Carlsen K. *(Denmark)*
Cash P. *(Australia)*
94 Champion T. *(France)*
111 Chang A. *(Canada)*
64 Chang M. *(USA)*
55 Chesnokov A. *(Russia)*
125 Clavet F. *(Spain)*
Conde J.A. *(Spain)*
Connell G. *(Canada)*
54 Corretja A. *(Spain)*
63 Costa A. *(Spain)*
106 Costa C. *(Spain)*
97 Courier J. *(USA)*
42 Cunha-Silva J. *(Portugal)*
40 Damm M. *(Czech Republic)*
Davids H.J. *(Netherlands)*
Davis S.E. *(USA)*
De Jager J-L. *(South Africa)*
Delgado J. *(Great Britain)*
107 Dewulf F. *(Belgium)*
Di Lucia D. *(USA)*
47 Draper S. *(Australia)*
46 Dreekmann H. *(Germany)*
Eagle J. *(Australia)*
49 Edberg S. *(Sweden)*
Ekerot D. *(Sweden)*
120 El Aynaoui Y. *(Morocco)*
92 Eltingh J. *(Netherlands)*
112 Enqvist T. *(Sweden)*
Ferreira E. *(South Africa)*
80 Ferreira W. *(South Africa)*
118 Fetterlein F. *(Denmark)*
95 Flach D. *(USA)*
Flach K. *(USA)*
127 Fleurian J-P. *(France)*
Florent A. *(Australia)*
50 Forget G. *(France)*
10 Foster A.L. *(Great Britain)*
4 Frana J. *(Argentina)*
109 Fromberg R. *(Australia)*
85 Furlan R. *(Italy)*
Galbraith P. *(USA)*
78 Gaudenzi A. *(Italy)*
123 Godwin N. *(South Africa)*
52 Goellner M. *(Germany)*
100 Golmard J. *(France)*
5 Goossens K. *(Belgium)*
88 Gould N. *(Great Britain)*
84 Grabb J. *(USA)*
75 Gustafsson M. *(Sweden)*
102 Haarhuis P. *(Netherlands)*
Hand P.T. *(Great Britain)*
Haygarth B. *(South Africa)*
66 Henman T. *(Great Britain)*
56 Hlasek J. *(Switzerland)*
74 Huet S. *(France)*
Humphries S. *(USA)*
Huning M. *(Germany)*
76 Ilie A. *(Australia)*
Ireland J. *(Australia)*
33 Ivanisevic G. *(Croatia)*
12 Jarryd A. *(Sweden)*
Jensen L.B. *(USA)*
Jensen M. *(USA)*
91 Johansson T. *(Sweden)*
Johnson D. *(USA)*
Jones K. *(USA)*
77 Joyce M. *(USA)*
65 Kafelnikov Y. *(Russia)*
Keil M. *(USA)*
27 Kempers T. *(Netherlands)*
Kilderry P. *(Australia)*
Kinnear K. *(USA)*
Kitinov A. *(MacEdonia)*
99 Knowles M. *(Bahamas)*
Koves G. *(Hungary)*
32 Krajicek R. *(Netherlands)*
Kratzmann A. *(Australia)*
Kronemann T. *(USA)*
9 Kroslak J. *(Slovakia)*
8 Kucera K. *(Slovakia)*
Kuhnen P. *(Germany)*
90 Kulti N. *(Sweden)*
72 Lapentti N. *(Ecuador)*
Lareau S. *(Canada)*
24 Larsson M. *(Sweden)*
Leach R. *(USA)*
Lucena M. *(USA)*
Macpherson D. *(Australia)*
MacPhie B. *(USA)*
Mandl G. *(Austria)*
37 Manta L. *(Switzerland)*
101 Mantilla F. *(Spain)*
Markovits L. *(Hungary)*
81 Martin T. *(USA)*
Matheson R. *(Great Britain)*
20 Matsuoka S. *(Japan)*
86 Medvedev A. *(Ukraine)*
70 Milligan L. *(Great Britain)*
Montana F. *(USA)*
36 Moya C. *(Spain)*
Muller G. *(South Africa)*
34 Nainkin D. *(South Africa)*
22 Nargiso D. *(Italy)*
61 Navarra M. *(Italy)*
25 Nestor D. *(Canada)*
Nijssen T. *(Netherlands)*
Norval P. *(South Africa)*
122 Noszaly S. *(Hungary)*
Noteboom S. *(Netherlands)*
58 Novak J. *(Czech Republic)*
Nyborg P. *(Sweden)*
O'Brien A. *(USA)*
39 Ogorodov O. *(Uzbekhistan)*
45 Olhovskiy A. *(Russia)*
82 Ondruska M. *(South Africa)*
Oosting M. *(Netherlands)*
13 Paes L. *(India)*
Pala P. *(Czech Republic)*
93 Palmer J. *(USA)*
104 Pereira N. *(Venezuela)*
115 Pescosolido S. *(Italy)*
14 Petchey M.R.J. *(Great Britain)*
3 Philippoussis M. *(Australia)*
Pimek L. *(Belgium)*
16 Pioline C. *(France)*
41 Pozzi G. *(Italy)*
79 Prinosil D. *(Germany)*
114 Radulescu A. *(Germany)*
43 Rafter P. *(Australia)*
Randall D. *(USA)*
119 Raoux G. *(France)*
2 Reneberg R.A. *(USA)*
57 Renzenbrink J. *(Germany)*
Richardson A.L. *(Great Britain)*
62 Rikl D. *(Czech Republic)*
Roig F. *(Spain)*
48 Rosset M. *(Switzerland)*
29 Rostagno D. *(USA)*
26 Rusedski G. *(Great Britain)*
19 Ruud C. *(Norway)*
1 Sampras P. *(USA)*
83 Sanchez E. *(Spain)*
31 Sanchez J. *(Spain)*
68 Sapsford D.E. *(Great Britain)*
18 Schalken S. *(Netherlands)*
15 Siemerink J. *(Netherlands)*
108 Spadea V. *(USA)*
Spinks T. *(Great Britain)*
121 Stafford G. *(South Africa)*
98 Stark J. *(USA)*
28 Steven B. *(New Zealand)*
17 Stich M. *(Germany)*
21 Stolle S. *(Australia)*
59 Stoltenberg J. *(Australia)*
Suk C. *(Czech Republic)*
Talbot B. *(South Africa)*
53 Tebbutt M. *(Australia)*
Thorne K. *(USA)*
51 Tillstrom M. *(Sweden)*
67 Tramacchi P. *(Australia)*
105 Ulihrach B. *(Czech Republic)*
44 Vacek D. *(Czech Republic)*
Van Emburgh G. *(USA)*
30 Van Herck J. *(Belgium)*
Van Rensburg C.J. *(South Africa)*
Vizner P. *(Czech Republic)*
60 Voinea A. *(Romania)*
38 Volkov A. *(Russia)*
Waite J. *(USA)*
110 Washington M. *(USA)*
117 Wheaton D. *(USA)*
11 Wilkinson C. *(Great Britain)*
73 Woodbridge T.A. *(Australia)*
23 Woodforde M. *(Australia)*
116 Woodruff C. *(USA)*

GIRLS

Andriyani Miss L. *(Indonesia)*
24 Barabanschikova Miss O. *(Belarus)*
31 Bernal Miss L. *(Paraguay)*
29 Black Miss C. *(Zimbabwe)*
26 Casoni Miss G. *(Italy)*
13 Castano Miss C. *(Columbia)*
11 Cho Miss Y-J. *(South Korea)*
35 Choudhury Miss J. *(Great Britain)*
49 Cocheteux Miss A. *(France)*
22 Curran Miss C. *(Eire)*
37 de Beer Miss S. *(South Africa)*
48 Dechy Miss N. *(France)*
16 Drake-Brockman Miss S.E. *(Australia)*
33 Ellwood Miss A. *(Australia)*
15 Gaviria Miss D. *(Peru)*
1 Grzybowska Miss M. *(Poland)*
25 Gubacsi Miss Z. *(Hungary)*
5 Hubnerova Miss N. *(Czech Republic)*
10 Inoue Miss M. *(Japan)*
21 Jagieniak Miss K. *(France)*
19 Janes Miss A. *(Great Britain)*
Jensen Miss A. *(Australia)*
57 Jeon Miss M. *(South Korea)*
17 Kleinova Miss S. *(Czech Republic)*
6 Koulikovskaya Miss E. *(Russia)*
53 Kovacevic Miss M. *(Croatia)*
43 Kovacic Miss S. *(Germany)*
Kurimay Miss A. *(Hungary)*
27 Latimer Miss L. *(Great Britain)*
62 Lehnhoff Miss J. *(USA)*
8 Lucic Miss M. *(Croatia)*
46 Marosi Miss K. *(Hungary)*
9 Mauresmo Miss A. *(France)*
36 Morigami Miss A. *(Japan)*
3 Nacuk Miss S. *(Yugoslavia)*
58 Ondraskova Miss Z. *(Czech Republic)*
Osman Miss J. *(Great Britain)*
56 Osterloh Miss L. *(USA)*
42 Palencia Miss P. *(Mexico)*
Pastikova Miss M. *(Czech Republic)*
7 Perkins Miss L. *(Great Britain)*
45 Popescu Miss C. *(Canada)*
51 Poutchek Miss T. *(Belarus)*
38 Radeljevic Miss A. *(Croatia)*
39 Reeves Miss S. *(USA)*
2 Rippner Miss A. *(USA)*
44 Roubanova Miss E. *(Great Britain)*
63 Sandu Miss R. *(Romania)*
64 Schnyder Miss P. *(Switzerland)*
41 Schonfeldova Miss J. *(Czech Republic)*
28 Schwarz Miss A. *(Switzerland)*
12 Sebova Miss A. *(Slovakia)*
59 Seljutina Miss I. *(Kazakstan)*
55 Serna Miss M. *(Spain)*
32 Sidot Miss A-G. *(France)*
18 Soukup Miss A. *(Canada)*
52 Srebotnik Miss K. *(Slovenia)*
14 Steck Miss J. *(South Africa)*
54 Straczy Miss K. *(Poland)*
50 Teperberg Miss R. *(Israel)*
20 Tokuda Miss K. *(USA)*
60 Tordoff Miss A. *(Great Britain)*
47 Triska Miss K. *(Sweden)*
23 Urickova Miss S. *(Slovakia)*
61 Valekova Miss Z. *(Slovakia)*
34 Volekova Miss G. *(Slovakia)*
30 White Miss M. *(USA)*
4 Wohr Miss J. *(Germany)*
40 Zuluaga Miss F. *(Columbia)*

BOYS

22 Abrams G. *(USA)*
10 Allegro Y. *(Switzerland)*
42 Allgauer F. *(Italy)*
28 Asturias A. *(Guatemala)*
38 Boroczky Z. *(Hungary)*
24 Bracciali D. *(Italy)*
19 Brandt J-R. *(Germany)*
58 Bryan B. *(USA)*
5 Cadart R. *(France)*
39 Capalik K. *(Bosnia-Herzegovina)*
27 Crabb J. *(Australia)*
41 Daniel M. *(Brazil)*
40 Di Pasquale A. *(France)*
51 Dickson S. *(Great Britain)*
63 Gaoni S. *(Australia)*
36 Gnjatovic N. *(Yugoslavia)*
45 Gonzalez F. *(Chile)*
3 Gregorc M. *(Slovenia)*
17 Grosjean S. *(France)*
49 Hadad A. *(Israel)*
62 Haran B. *(Great Britain)*
32 Hellstrom M. *(Sweden)*
14 Herbert W. *(Great Britain)*
15 Horna L. *(Peru)*
34 Hui J. *(Hong Kong)*
47 Ivanov-Smolenski K. *(Russia)*
26 Jancso M. *(Hungary)*
43 Kim A. *(USA)*
35 Kim D-H. *(South Korea)*
52 Kim K. *(USA)*
23 Krajan Z. *(Croatia)*
53 Kralert P. *(Czech Republic)*
57 Kratochvil M. *(Switzerland)*
33 Lee M. *(Great Britain)*
20 Lee S-H. *(South Korea)*
12 Levy H. *(Israel)*
46 Ljubicic I. *(Croatia)*
55 Mankad H. *(India)*
2 Massu N. *(Chile)*
18 Navawongse C. *(Thailand)*
44 Osterbrink B. *(Germany)*
30 Ouahabi T. *(Morocco)*
7 Parmar A. *(Great Britain)*
21 Pender S.T. *(Great Britain)*
61 Pequery J. *(France)*
25 Puerta M. *(Argentina)*
8 Rake R. *(USA)*
48 Rehnqvist B.C. *(Sweden)*
54 Roberts D. *(South Africa)*
9 Robichaud J. *(Canada)*
6 Romero Y. *(Venezuela)*
60 Russell M. *(USA)*
31 Sanchez M. *(Mexico)*
11 Sarstrand M. *(Sweden)*
59 Sciortino D. *(Italy)*
29 Sherwood D. *(Great Britain)*
56 Srichaphan P. *(Thailand)*
4 Sta-Cruz D. *(Philippines)*
1 Tabara M. *(Czech Republic)*
50 Turkovic M. *(Slovakia)*
37 Vik R. *(Czech Republic)*
16 Voltchkov V. *(Belarus)*
64 Wessels P. *(Netherlands)*
13 Whitehouse W. *(South Africa)*

Bold figures denote position in Singles Draw

Holder: P. SAMPRAS

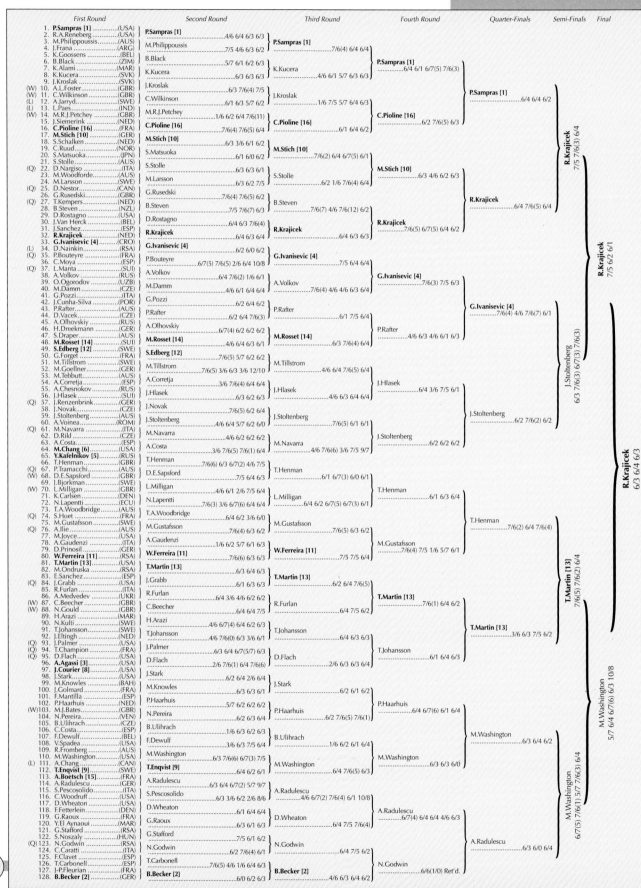

First Round	Second Round	Third Round	Fourth Round	Quarter-Finals	Semi-Finals	Final

1. **P.Sampras [1]** ....(USA)
2. R.A.Reneberg ....(USA)
3. M.Philippoussis.........(AUS)
4. J.Frana ....(ARG)
5. K.Goossens ....(BEL)
6. B.Black ....(ZIM)
7. K.Alami ....(MAR)
8. K.Kucera ....(SVK)
9. J.Kroslak ....(SVK)
(W) 10. A.L.Foster ....(GBR)
(W) 11. C.Wilkinson ....(GBR)
(L) 12. A.Jarryd ....(SWE)
(L) 13. L.Paes ....(IND)
(W) 14. M.R.J.Petchey ....(GBR)
15. J.Siemerink ....(NED)
16. **C.Pioline [16]** ....(FRA)
17. **M.Stich [10]** ....(GER)
18. S.Schalken ....(NED)
19. C.Ruud ....(NOR)
20. S.Matsuoka ....(JPN)
21. S.Stolle ....(AUS)
(Q) 22. D.Nargiso ....(ITA)
23. M.Woodforde ....(AUS)
24. M.Larsson ....(SWE)
(Q) 25. D.Nestor ....(CAN)
26. G.Rusedski ....(GBR)
(Q) 27. T.Kempers ....(NED)
28. B.Steven ....(NZL)
29. D.Rostagno ....(USA)
30. J.Van Herck ....(BEL)
31. J.Sanchez ....(ESP)
32. **R.Krajicek** ....(NED)
33. **G.Ivanisevic [4]** ....(CRO)
(L) 34. D.Nainkin ....(RSA)
(Q) 35. P.Bouteyre ....(FRA)
36. C.Moya ....(ESP)
(Q) 37. L.Manta ....(SUI)
38. A.Volkov ....(RUS)
39. O.Ogorodov ....(UZB)
40. M.Damm ....(CZE)
41. G.Pozzi ....(ITA)
42. J.Cunha-Silva ....(POR)
43. P.Rafter ....(AUS)
44. D.Vacek ....(CZE)
45. A.Olhovskiy ....(RUS)
46. H.Dreekmann ....(GER)
47. S.Draper ....(AUS)
48. **M.Rosset [14]** ....(SUI)
49. **S.Edberg [12]** ....(SWE)
50. G.Forget ....(FRA)
51. M.Tillstrom ....(SWE)
52. M.Goellner ....(GER)
53. M.Tebbutt ....(AUS)
54. A.Corretja ....(ESP)
55. A.Chesnokov ....(RUS)
56. J.Hlasek ....(SUI)
(Q) 57. J.Renzenbrink ....(GER)
58. J.Novak ....(CZE)
59. J.Stoltenberg ....(AUS)
60. A.Voinea ....(ROM)
(Q) 61. M.Navarra ....(ITA)
62. D.Rikl ....(CZE)
63. A.Costa ....(ESP)
64. **M.Chang [6]** ....(USA)
65. **Y.Kafelnikov [5]** ....(RUS)
66. T.Henman ....(GBR)
(Q) 67. P.Tramacchi ....(AUS)
(W) 68. D.E.Sapsford ....(GBR)
69. J.Bjorkman ....(SWE)
(W) 70. L.Milligan ....(GBR)
71. K.Carlsen ....(DEN)
72. N.Lapentti ....(ECU)
73. T.A.Woodbridge ....(AUS)
(Q) 74. S.Huet ....(FRA)
75. M.Gustafsson ....(SWE)
(Q) 76. A.Ilie ....(AUS)
77. M.Joyce ....(USA)
78. A.Gaudenzi ....(ITA)
79. D.Prinosil ....(GER)
80. **W.Ferreira [11]** ....(RSA)
81. **T.Martin [13]**.............(USA)
82. M.Ondruska ....(RSA)
83. E.Sanchez ....(ESP)
(Q) 84. J.Grabb ....(USA)
85. R.Furlan ....(ITA)
86. A.Medvedev ....(UKR)
(W) 87. C.Beecher ....(GBR)
(W) 88. N.Gould ....(GBR)
89. H.Arazi ....(MAR)
90. N.Kulti ....(SWE)
91. T.Johansson ....(SWE)
92. J.Eltingh ....(NED)
(Q) 93. J.Palmer ....(USA)
(Q) 94. T.Champion ....(FRA)
(Q) 95. D.Flach ....(USA)
96. **A.Agassi [3]** ....(USA)
97. **J.Courier [8]** ....(USA)
98. J.Stark ....(USA)
99. M.Knowles ....(BAH)
100. J.Golmard ....(FRA)
101. F.Mantilla ....(ESP)
102. P.Haarhuis ....(NED)
(W)103. M.J.Bates ....(GBR)
104. N.Pereira ....(VEN)
105. B.Ulihrach ....(CZE)
106. C.Costa ....(ESP)
107. F.Dewulf ....(BEL)
108. V.Spadea ....(USA)
109. R.Fromberg ....(AUS)
110. M.Washington ....(USA)
(L) 111. A.Chang ....(CAN)
112. **T.Enqvist [9]** ....(SWE)
113. **A.Boetsch [15]** ....(FRA)
114. A.Radulescu ....(GER)
115. S.Pescosolido ....(ITA)
116. C.Woodruff ....(USA)
117. D.Wheaton ....(USA)
118. F.Fetterlein ....(DEN)
119. G.Raoux ....(FRA)
120. Y.El Aynaoui ....(MAR)
121. G.Stafford ....(RSA)
122. S.Noszaly ....(HUN)
(Q)123. N.Godwin ....(RSA)
124. C.Caratti ....(ITA)
125. F.Clavet ....(ESP)
126. T.Carbonell ....(ESP)
127. J-P.Fleurian ....(FRA)
128. **B.Becker [2]** ....(GER)

Second Round

P.Sampras [1] 4/6 6/4 6/3 6/3
M.Philippoussis 7/5 4/6 6/3 6/2
B.Black 5/7 6/1 6/2 6/3
K.Kucera 6/3 6/3 6/3
J.Kroslak ....6/3 7/6(4) 7/5
C.Wilkinson 6/1 6/3 5/7 6/2
M.R.J.Petchey ....1/6 6/2 6/4 7/6(11)
C.Pioline [16] ....7/6(4) 7/6(5) 6/4
M.Stich [10] 6/3 3/6 6/1 6/2
S.Matsuoka 6/1 6/0 6/2
S.Stolle 6/3 6/3 6/1
M.Larsson 6/3 6/2 7/5
G.Rusedski ....7/6(4) 7/6(5) 6/2
B.Steven ....7/5 7/6(7) 6/3
D.Rostagno ....6/4 6/3 7/6(4)
R.Krajicek 6/4 6/3 6/4
G.Ivanisevic [4] 6/2 6/0 6/2
P.Bouteyre ....6/7(5) 7/6(5) 2/6 6/4 10/8
A.Volkov ....6/4 7/6(2) 1/6 6/1
M.Damm 4/6 6/1 6/4 6/3
G.Pozzi 6/2 6/4 6/2
P.Rafter ....6/2 6/4 7/6(3)
A.Olhovskiy ....6/7(4) 6/2 6/2 6/2
M.Rosset [14] 4/6 6/4 6/3 6/1
S.Edberg [12] ....7/6(5) 5/7 6/2 6/2
M.Tillstrom ....7/6(5) 3/6 6/3 3/6 12/10
A.Corretja ....3/6 7/6(4) 6/4 6/4
J.Hlasek 6/3 6/2 6/3
J.Novak ....7/6(5) 6/2 6/4
J.Stoltenberg 4/6 6/4 5/7 6/2 6/0
M.Navarra 4/6 6/2 6/2 6/2
A.Costa ....3/6 7/6(5) 7/6(1) 6/4
T.Henman ....7/6(6) 6/3 6/7(2) 4/6 7/5
D.E.Sapsford 7/5 6/4 6/3
L.Milligan 4/6 6/1 2/6 7/5 6/4
N.Lapentti ....7/6(3) 3/6 6/7(6) 6/4 6/4
T.A.Woodbridge 6/4 6/2 3/6 6/0
M.Gustafsson ....7/6(4) 6/3 6/2
A.Gaudenzi 1/6 6/2 5/7 6/1 6/3
W.Ferreira [11] ....7/6(6) 6/3 6/4
T.Martin [13] 6/3 6/4 6/3
J.Grabb 6/1 6/3 6/3
R.Furlan 6/4 3/6 4/6 6/2 6/2
C.Beecher 6/4 6/4 7/5
H.Arazi ....4/6 6/7(4) 6/4 6/2 6/3
T.Johansson ....4/6 7/6(0) 6/3 3/6 6/1
J.Palmer ....6/3 6/4 6/7(5/7) 6/3
D.Flach ....2/6 7/6(1) 6/4 7/6(6)
J.Stark 6/2 6/4 2/6 6/4
M.Knowles 6/3 6/3 6/1
P.Haarhuis 5/7 6/2 6/2 6/2
N.Pereira 6/2 6/3 6/4
B.Ulihrach 1/6 6/3 6/2 6/3
F.Dewulf 3/6 6/3 7/5 6/4
M.Washington ....6/3 7/6(6) 6/7(3) 7/5
T.Enqvist [9] 6/4 6/2 6/1
A.Radulescu ....6/3 6/4 6/7(2) 5/7 9/7
S.Pescosolido 6/3 3/6 6/2 2/6 8/6
D.Wheaton 6/1 6/4 6/4
G.Raoux 7/5 6/1 6/2
G.Stafford 7/5 6/1 6/2
N.Godwin ....6/2 7/6(4) 6/7
T.Carbonell ....7/6(5) 4/6 1/6 6/4 6/3
B.Becker [2] 6/0 6/2 6/3

Third Round

P.Sampras [1] ....7/6(4) 6/4 6/4
K.Kucera 4/6 6/1 5/7 6/3 6/3
C.Pioline [16] 6/1 6/4 6/2
M.Stich [10] ....7/6(2) 6/4 6/7(5) 6/1
S.Stolle ....6/2 1/6 7/6(4) 6/4
B.Steven ....7/6(7) 4/6 7/6(12) 6/1
R.Krajicek 6/4 6/3 6/3
G.Ivanisevic [4] 7/5 6/4 6/3
A.Volkov ....7/6(4) 4/6 4/6 6/3 6/4
P.Rafter 6/1 7/5 6/4
M.Rosset [14] ....6/3 7/6(4) 6/4
M.Tillstrom ....4/6 6/4 7/6(5) 6/4
J.Hlasek 4/6 6/3 6/4 6/4
J.Stoltenberg ....7/6(5) 6/1 6/1
M.Navarra ....4/6 7/6(6) 3/6 7/5 9/7
T.Henman ....6/1 6/7(3) 6/0 6/1
L.Milligan ....6/4 6/2 6/7(5) 7/6(3) 6/1
M.Gustafsson ....7/6(5) 6/3 6/2
W.Ferreira [11] 7/5 7/5 6/4
T.Martin [13] ....6/2 2/6 4/7 7/6(5)
R.Furlan 6/4 7/5 6/4
T.Johansson 6/4 6/3 6/3
D.Flach 2/6 6/3 6/3 6/4
J.Stark 6/2 6/1 6/2
P.Haarhuis ....6/2 7/6(5) 7/6(1)
B.Ulihrach 1/6 6/2 6/1 6/4
M.Washington ....6/4 7/6(5) 6/3
A.Radulescu ....4/6 6/7(2) 7/6(4) 6/1 10/8
D.Wheaton ....6/4 7/5 7/6(4)
N.Godwin 6/4 7/5 6/2
B.Becker [2] 4/6 6/3 6/4 6/2

Fourth Round

P.Sampras [1] ....6/4 6/1 6/7(5) 7/6(3)
C.Pioline [16] ....6/2 7/6(5) 6/3
M.Stich [10] 6/3 4/6 6/2 6/3
R.Krajicek ....7/6(5) 6/7(5) 6/4 6/2
G.Ivanisevic [4] ....7/6(3) 7/5 6/3
P.Rafter 4/6 6/3 4/6 6/1 6/3
J.Hlasek 6/4 3/6 7/5 6/1
J.Stoltenberg 6/2 6/2 6/2
T.Henman 6/1 6/3 6/4
M.Gustafsson ....7/6(4) 7/5 1/6 5/7 6/1
T.Martin [13] ....7/6(1) 6/4 6/2
T.Johansson 6/1 6/4 6/3
M.Washington 6/3 6/3 6/0
A.Radulescu ....6/7(4) 6/4 6/4 4/6 6/3
N.Godwin ....6/6(1/0) Ret'd.

Quarter-Finals

P.Sampras [1] 6/4 6/4 6/2
R.Krajicek ....6/4 7/6(5) 6/4
G.Ivanisevic [4] ....7/6(4) 4/6 7/6(7) 6/1
J.Stoltenberg ....6/2 7/6(2) 6/2
T.Henman ....7/6(2) 6/4 7/6(4)
T.Martin [13] 3/6 6/3 7/5 6/2
M.Washington 6/3 6/4 6/2
A.Radulescu 6/3 6/0 6/4

Semi-Finals

R.Krajicek ....7/5 7/6(3) 6/4
J.Stoltenberg ....6/3 7/6(3) 6/7(3) 7/6(3)
T.Martin [13] ....7/6(5) 7/6(2) 6/4
M.Washington ....5/7 6/4 6/7(6) 6/3 10/8

Final

R.Krajicek 7/5 6/2 6/1
M.Washington ....6/7(5) 7/6(1) 5/7 7/6(3) 6/4

R.Krajicek 6/3 6/4 6/3

Holders: T. A. Woodbridge and M. Woodforde

The winners become the holders, for the year only, of the CHALLENGE CUPS presented by the OXFORD UNIVERSITY LAWN TENNIS CLUB and the late SIR HERBERT WILBERFORCE respectively. The winners receive silver replicas of the two Challenge Cups. A silver salver is presented to each of the runners-up, and a bronze medal to each defeated semi-finalist.

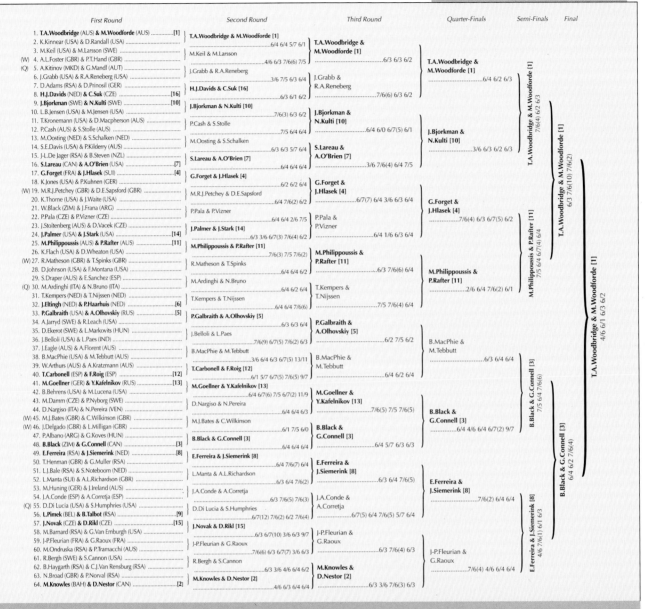

First Round	Second Round	Third Round	Quarter-Finals	Semi-Finals	Final
1. T.A.Woodbridge (AUS) & M.Woodforde (AUS) [1]	T.A.Woodbridge & M.Woodforde [1]				
2. K.Kinnear (USA) & D.Randall (USA)	6/4 6/4 5/7 6/1	T.A.Woodbridge & M.Woodforde [1]			
3. M.Keil (USA) & M.Larsson (SWE)	M.Keil & M.Larsson	6/3 6/3 6/2			
(W) 4. A.L.Foster (GBR) & P.T.Hand (GBR)	4/6 6/3 7/6(6) 7/5		T.A.Woodbridge & M.Woodforde [1]		
(Q) 5. A.Kitinov (MKD) & G.Mandl (AUT)	J.Grabb & R.A.Reneberg		6/4 6/2 6/3		
6. J.Grabb (USA) & R.A.Reneberg (USA)	3/6 7/5 6/3 6/4	J.Grabb & R.A.Reneberg			
7. D.Adams (RSA) & D.Prinosil (GER)	H.J.Davids & C.Suk [16]	7/6(6) 6/3 6/2			
8. H.J.Davids (NED) & C.Suk (CZE) [16]	6/3 6/1 6/2			T.A.Woodbridge & M.Woodforde [1]	
9. J.Bjorkman (SWE) & N.Kulti (SWE) [10]	J.Bjorkman & N.Kulti [10]			7/6(4) 6/2 6/3	
10. L.B.Jensen (USA) & M.Jensen (USA)	7/6(3) 6/3 6/2	J.Bjorkman & N.Kulti [10]			
11. T.Kronemann (USA) & D.Macpherson (AUS)	P.Cash & S.Stolle	6/4 6/0 6/7(5) 6/1			
12. P.Cash (AUS) & S.Stolle (AUS)	7/5 6/4 6/4		J.Bjorkman & N.Kulti [10]		
13. M.Oosting (NED) & S.Schalken (NED)	M.Oosting & S.Schalken		3/6 6/3 6/2 6/3		
14. S.E.Davis (USA) & P.Kilderry (AUS)	6/3 6/3 5/7 6/4	S.Lareau & A.O'Brien [7]			
15. J-L.De Jager (RSA) & B.Steven (NZL)	S.Lareau & A.O'Brien [7]	3/6 7/6(4) 6/4 7/5			
16. S.Lareau (CAN) & A.O'Brien (USA) [7]	6/4 6/4 6/4				
17. G.Forget (FRA) & J.Hlasek (SUI) [4]	G.Forget & J.Hlasek [4]				T.A.Woodbridge & M.Woodforde [1]
18. K.Jones (USA) & P.Kuhnen (GER)	6/2 6/2 6/4	G.Forget & J.Hlasek [4]			6/3 7/6(10) 7/6(2)
(W) 19. M.R.J.Petchey (GBR) & D.E.Sapsford (GBR)	M.R.J.Petchey & D.E.Sapsford	6/7(7) 6/4 3/6 6/4 6/4			
20. K.Thorne (USA) & J.Waite (USA)	6/4 7/6(2) 6/2		G.Forget & J.Hlasek [4]		
21. W.Black (ZIM) & J.Frana (ARG)	P.Pala & P.Vizner		7/6(4) 6/3 6/7(5) 6/2		
22. P.Pala (CZE) & P.Vizner (CZE)	6/4 6/4 2/6 7/5	P.Pala & P.Vizner			
23. J.Stoltenberg (AUS) & D.Vacek (CZE)	J.Palmer & J.Stark [14]	6/4 1/6 6/3 6/4			
24. J.Palmer (USA) & J.Stark (USA) [14]	6/3 3/6 6/7(3) 7/6(4) 6/2			M.Philippoussis & P.Rafter [11]	
25. M.Philippoussis (AUS) & P.Rafter (AUS) [11]	M.Philippoussis & P.Rafter [11]			7/5 6/4 6/7(4) 6/4	
26. K.Flach (USA) & D.Wheaton (USA)	7/6(3) 7/5 7/6(2)	M.Philippoussis & P.Rafter [11]			
(W) 27. R.Matheson (GBR) & T.Spinks (GBR)	R.Matheson & T.Spinks	6/3 7/6(6) 6/4			
28. D.Johnson (USA) & F.Montana (USA)	6/4 6/4 6/2		M.Philippoussis & P.Rafter [11]		
29. S.Draper (AUS) & E.Sanchez (ESP)	M.Ardinghi & N.Bruno		2/6 6/4 7/6(2) 6/1		
(Q) 30. M.Ardinghi (ITA) & N.Bruno (ITA)	6/4 6/2 6/4	T.Kempers & T.Nijssen			
31. T.Kempers (NED) & T.Nijssen (NED)	T.Kempers & T.Nijssen	7/5 7/6(4) 6/4			
32. J.Eltingh (NED) & P.Haarhuis (NED) [6]	6/4 6/4 7/6(6)				
33. P.Galbraith (USA) & A.Olhovskiy (RUS) [5]	P.Galbraith & A.Olhovskiy [5]				M.Philippoussis & P.Rafter [11]
34. A.Jarryd (SWE) & R.Leach (USA)	6/3 6/3 6/4	P.Galbraith & A.Olhovskiy [5]			6/4 6/1 6/3 6/2
35. D.Ekerot (SWE) & L.Markovits (HUN)	J.Belloli & L.Paes	6/2 7/5 6/2			
36. J.Belloli (USA) & L.Paes (IND)	7/6(9) 6/7(5) 7/6(2) 6/3		B.MacPhie & M.Tebbutt		
37. J.Eagle (AUS) & A.Florent (AUS)	B.MacPhie & M.Tebbutt		6/3 6/4 6/4		
38. B.MacPhie (USA) & M.Tebbutt (AUS)	3/6 6/4 6/4 6/7(5) 13/11	B.MacPhie & M.Tebbutt			
39. W.Arthurs (AUS) & A.Kratzmann (AUS)	T.Carbonell & F.Roig [12]	6/4 6/2 6/4			
40. T.Carbonell (ESP) & F.Roig (ESP) [12]	6/1 5/7 6/7(5) 7/6(5) 9/7			B.Black & G.Connell [3]	
41. M.Goellner (GER) & Y.Kafelnikov (RUS) [13]	M.Goellner & Y.Kafelnikov [13]			7/5 6/4 7/6(6)	
42. B.Behrens (USA) & M.Lucena (USA)	6/4 6/7(6) 7/5 6/7(2) 11/9	M.Goellner & Y.Kafelnikov [13]			
43. M.Damm (CZE) & P.Nyborg (SWE)	D.Nargiso & N.Pereira	7/6(5) 7/5 7/6(5)			
44. D.Nargiso (ITA) & N.Pereira (VEN)	6/4 6/4 6/3		B.Black & G.Connell [3]		
(W) 45. M.J.Bates (GBR) & C.Wilkinson (GBR)	M.J.Bates & C.Wilkinson		6/4 4/6 6/4 6/7(2) 9/7		
(W) 46. J.Delgado (GBR) & L.Milligan (GBR)	6/1 7/5 6/0	B.Black & G.Connell [3]			
47. P.Albano (ARG) & G.Koves (HUN)	B.Black & G.Connell [3]	6/4 5/7 6/3 6/3			
48. B.Black (ZIM) & G.Connell (CAN) [3]	6/4 6/4 6/4				
49. E.Ferreira (RSA) & J.Siemerink (NED) [8]	E.Ferreira & J.Siemerink [8]			B.Black & G.Connell [3]	
50. T.Henman (GBR) & G.Muller (RSA)	6/4 7/6(7) 6/4	E.Ferreira & J.Siemerink [8]		6/4 6/2 7/6(4)	
51. L.J.Bale (RSA) & S.Noteboom (NED)	L.Manta & A.L.Richardson	6/3 6/4 7/6(5)			
52. L.Manta (SUI) & A.L.Richardson (GBR)	6/3 6/7(7) 7/6(2)		E.Ferreira & J.Siemerink [8]		
53. M.Huning (GER) & J.Ireland (AUS)	J.A.Conde & A.Corretja		7/6(2) 6/4 6/4		
54. J.A.Conde (ESP) & A.Corretja (ESP)	6/3 7/6(5) 7/6(3)	J.A.Conde & A.Corretja			
(Q) 55. D.Di Lucia (USA) & S.Humphries (USA)	D.Di Lucia & S.Humphries	6/7(5) 6/4 7/6(5) 5/7 6/4			
56. L.Pimek (BEL) & B.Talbot (RSA) [9]	6/7(12) 7/6(2) 6/2 7/6(4)			E.Ferreira & J.Siemerink [8]	
57. J.Novak (CZE) & D.Rikl (CZE) [15]	J.Novak & D.Rikl [15]			4/6 7/6(1) 6/1 6/3	
58. M.Barnard (RSA) & G.Van Emburgh (USA)	6/3 6/7(10) 3/6 6/3 9/7	J-P.Fleurian & G.Raoux			
59. J-P.Fleurian (FRA) & G.Raoux (FRA)	J-P.Fleurian & G.Raoux	6/3 7/6(4) 6/3			
60. M.Ondruska (RSA) & P.Tramacchi (AUS)	7/6(6) 6/4 6/7(3) 7/6 6/3		J-P.Fleurian & G.Raoux		
61. R.Bergh (SWE) & S.Cannon (USA)	R.Bergh & S.Cannon		7/6(4) 4/6 6/4 6/4		
62. B.Haygarth (RSA) & C.J.Van Rensburg (RSA)	6/3 3/6 4/6 6/4 6/2	M.Knowles & D.Nestor [2]			
63. N.Broad (GBR) & P.Norval (RSA)	M.Knowles & D.Nestor [2]	6/3 3/6 7/6(3) 6/3			
64. M.Knowles (BAH) & D.Nestor (CAN) [2]	4/6 6/3 6/4 6/4				

Heavy type denotes seeded players. The figure in brackets against names denotes the order in which they have been seeded. (W) = Wild card. (Q) = Qualifier. (L) = Lucky loser.

The matches are the best of five sets

THE 45 AND OVER GENTLEMEN'S INVITATION DOUBLES

Holders: J. D. Newcombe and A. D. Roche

The winners become the holders, for the year only, of a Cup presented by The All England Lawn Tennis and Croquet Club. The winners receive miniature silver salvers. A silver medal is presented to each of the runners-up.

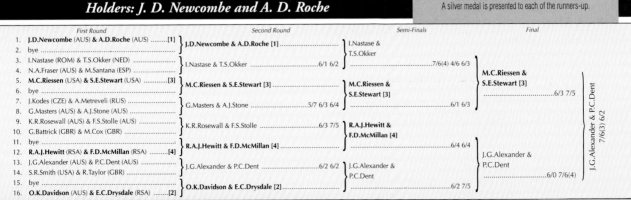

First Round	Second Round	Semi-Finals	Final
1. J.D.Newcombe (AUS) & A.D.Roche (AUS) [1]	J.D.Newcombe & A.D.Roche [1]	I.Nastase & T.S.Okker	
2. bye			
3. I.Nastase (ROM) & T.S.Okker (NED)	I.Nastase & T.S.Okker 6/1 6/2	7/6(4) 4/6 6/3	
4. N.A.Fraser (AUS) & M.Santana (ESP)			M.C.Riessen & S.E.Stewart [3]
5. M.C.Riessen (USA) & S.E.Stewart (USA) [3]	M.C.Riessen & S.E.Stewart [3]	M.C.Riessen & S.E.Stewart [3]	
6. bye			
7. I.Kodes (CZE) & A.Metreveli (RUS)	G.Masters & A.J.Stone 5/7 6/3 6/4	6/1 6/3	6/3 7/5
8. G.Masters (AUS) & A.J.Stone (AUS)			
9. K.R.Rosewall (AUS) & F.S.Stolle (AUS)	K.R.Rosewall & F.S.Stolle 6/3 7/5	R.A.J.Hewitt & F.D.McMillan [4]	
10. G.Battrick (GBR) & M.Cox (GBR)			
11. bye		6/4 6/4	
12. R.A.J.Hewitt (RSA) & F.D.McMillan (RSA) [4]	R.A.J.Hewitt & F.D.McMillan [4]		J.G.Alexander & P.C.Dent
13. J.G.Alexander (AUS) & P.C.Dent (AUS)	J.G.Alexander & P.C.Dent 6/2 6/2	J.G.Alexander & P.C.Dent	
14. S.R.Smith (USA) & R.Taylor (GBR)			6/0 7/6(4)
15. bye		6/2 7/5	
16. O.K.Davidson (AUS) & E.C.Drysdale (RSA) [2]	O.K.Davidson & E.C.Drysdale [2]		

Final: J.G.Alexander & P.C.Dent 7/6(3) 6/2

Heavy type denotes seeded players. The figure in brackets against names denotes the order in which they have been seeded.

The matches are the best of three sets

Holder: Miss S. Graf

The winner becomes the holder, for the year only, of the CHALLENGE TROPHY presented by The All England Lawn Tennis and Croquet Club. The winner receives a silver replica of the Trophy. A silver salver is presented to the runner-up and a bronze medal to each defeated semi-finalist.

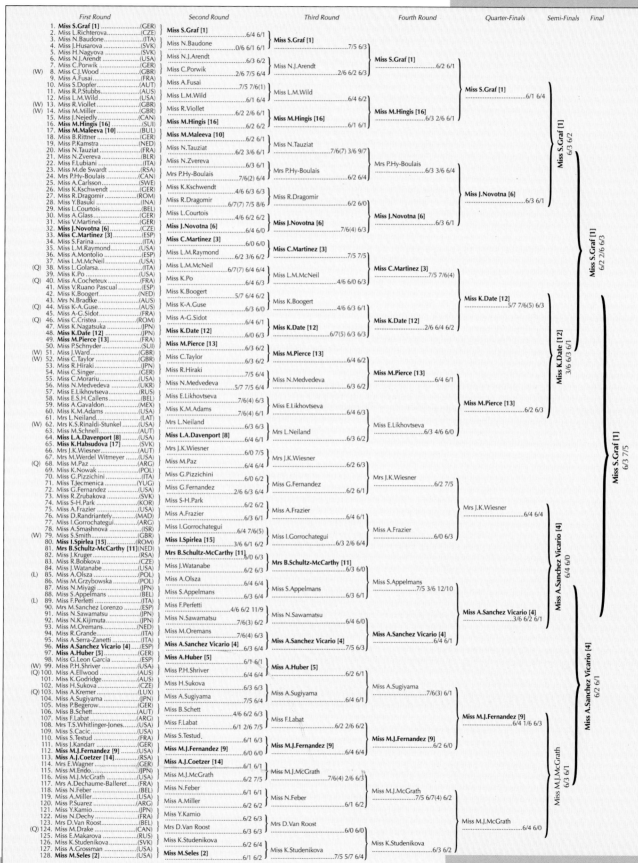

First Round

1. Miss S.Graf [1] ......(GER)
2. Miss L.Richterova ......(CZE)
3. Miss N.Baudone ......(ITA)
4. Miss J.Husarova ......(SVK)
5. Miss H.Nagyova ......(SVK)
6. Miss N.J.Arendt ......(USA)
7. Miss C.Porwik ......(GER)
(W) 8. Miss C.J.Wood ......(GBR)
9. Miss A.Fusai ......(FRA)
10. Miss S.Dopfer ......(AUT)
11. Miss R.P.Stubbs ......(AUS)
12. Miss L.M.Wild ......(USA)
(W) 13. Miss R.Viollet ......(GBR)
(W) 14. Miss M.Miller ......(GBR)
15. Miss J.Nejedly ......(CAN)
16. Miss M.Hingis [16] ......(SUI)
17. Miss M.Maleeva [10] ......(BUL)
18. Miss B.Rittner ......(GER)
19. Miss P.Kamstra ......(NED)
20. Miss N.Tauziat ......(FRA)
21. Miss N.Zvereva ......(BLR)
22. Miss F.Lubiani ......(ITA)
23. Miss M.de Swardt ......(RSA)
24. Miss P.Hy-Boulais ......(CAN)
25. Miss A.Carlsson ......(SWE)
26. Miss K.Kschwendt ......(GER)
27. Miss R.Dragomir ......(ROM)
28. Miss Y.Basuki ......(INA)
29. Miss L.Courtois ......(BEL)
30. Miss A.Glass ......(GER)
31. Miss V.Martinek ......(GER)
32. Miss J.Novotna [6] ......(CZE)
33. Miss C.Martinez [3] ......(ESP)
34. Miss S.Farina ......(ITA)
35. Miss L.M.Raymond ......(USA)
36. Miss A.Montolio ......(ESP)
37. Miss L.M.McNeil ......(USA)
(Q) 38. Miss L.Golarsa ......(ITA)
39. Miss K.Po ......(USA)
(Q) 40. Miss A.Cocheteux ......(FRA)
41. Miss V.Ruano Pascual ......(ESP)
42. Miss K.Boogert ......(NED)
43. Mrs N.Bradtke ......(AUS)
(Q) 44. Miss K-A.Guse ......(AUS)
45. Miss A-G.Sidot ......(FRA)
(Q) 46. Miss C.Cristea ......(ROM)
47. Miss K.Nagatsuka ......(JPN)
48. Miss K.Date [12] ......(JPN)
49. Miss M.Pierce [13] ......(FRA)
50. Miss P.Schnyder ......(SUI)
(W) 51. Miss J.Ward ......(GBR)
(W) 52. Miss C.Taylor ......(GBR)
53. Miss R.Hiraki ......(JPN)
54. Miss C.Singer ......(GER)
55. Miss C.Morariu ......(USA)
56. Miss N.Medvedeva ......(UKR)
57. Miss E.Likhovtseva ......(RUS)
58. Miss E.S.H.Callens ......(BEL)
59. Miss A.Gavaldon ......(MEX)
60. Miss K.M.Adams ......(USA)
61. Miss L.Neiland ......(LAT)
(W) 62. Mrs K.S.Rinaldi-Stunkel ......(USA)
63. Miss M.Schnell ......(AUT)
64. Miss L.A.Davenport [8] ......(USA)
65. Miss K.Habsudova [17] ......(SVK)
66. Mrs J.K.Wiesner ......(AUT)
67. Miss M.Werdel Witmeyer ......(USA)
(Q) 68. Miss M.Paz ......(ARG)
69. Miss K.Nowak ......(POL)
70. Miss G.Pizzichini ......(ITA)
71. Miss T.Jecmenica ......(YUG)
72. Miss G.Fernandez ......(USA)
73. Miss R.Zrubakova ......(SVK)
74. Miss S-H.Park ......(KOR)
75. Miss A.Frazier ......(USA)
76. Miss D.Randriantefy ......(MAD)
77. Miss I.Gorrochategui ......(ARG)
78. Miss A.Smashnova ......(ISR)
(W) 79. Miss S.Smith ......(GBR)
80. Miss I.Spirlea [15] ......(ROM)
81. Mrs B.Schultz-McCarthy [11] ......(NED)
82. Miss J.Kruger ......(RSA)
83. Miss R.Bobkova ......(CZE)
84. Miss J.Watanabe ......(USA)
(L) 85. Miss A.Olsza ......(POL)
86. Miss M.Grzybowska ......(POL)
87. Miss N.Miyagi ......(JPN)
88. Miss S.Appelmans ......(BEL)
(L) 89. Miss F.Perfetti ......(ITA)
90. Mrs M.Sanchez Lorenzo ......(ESP)
91. Miss N.Sawamatsu ......(JPN)
92. Miss N.K.Kijimuta ......(JPN)
93. Miss M.Oremans ......(NED)
94. Miss R.Grande ......(ITA)
95. Miss A.Serra-Zanetti ......(ITA)
96. Miss A.Sanchez Vicario [4] ......(ESP)
97. Miss A.Huber [5] ......(GER)
98. Miss G.Leon Garcia ......(ESP)
(W) 99. Miss P.H.Shriver ......(USA)
(Q) 100. Miss A.Ellwood ......(AUS)
101. Miss K.Godridge ......(AUS)
102. Miss H.Sukova ......(CZE)
(Q) 103. Miss A.Kremer ......(LUX)
104. Miss A.Sugiyama ......(JPN)
105. Miss P.Begerow ......(GER)
106. Miss B.Schett ......(AUT)
107. Miss F.Labat ......(ARG)
108. Miss T.S.Whitlinger-Jones ......(USA)
109. Miss S.Cacic ......(USA)
110. Miss S.Testud ......(FRA)
111. Miss J.Kandarr ......(GER)
112. Miss M.J.Fernandez [9] ......(USA)
113. Miss A.J.Coetzer [14] ......(RSA)
114. Mrs E.Wagner ......(GER)
115. Miss M.Endo ......(JPN)
116. Miss M.J.McGrath ......(USA)
117. Mrs A.Dechaume-Balleret ......(FRA)
118. Miss N.Feber ......(BEL)
119. Miss A.Miller ......(USA)
120. Miss P.Suarez ......(ARG)
121. Miss Y.Kamio ......(JPN)
122. Miss N.Dechy ......(FRA)
123. Mrs D.Van Roost ......(BEL)
(Q) 124. Miss M.Drake ......(CAN)
125. Miss E.Makarova ......(RUS)
126. Miss K.Studenikova ......(SVK)
127. Miss A.Grossman ......(USA)
128. Miss M.Seles [2] ......(USA)

Second Round

- Miss S.Graf [1] — 6/4 6/1
- Miss N.Baudone — 0/6 6/1 6/1
- Miss N.J.Arendt — 6/3 6/2
- Miss C.Porwik — 2/6 7/5 6/4
- Miss A.Fusai — 7/5 7/6(1)
- Miss L.M.Wild — 6/1 6/1
- Miss R.Viollet — 6/2 2/6 6/1
- Miss M.Hingis [16] — 6/2 6/2
- Miss M.Maleeva [10] — 6/2 6/1
- Miss N.Tauziat — 6/2 3/6 6/1
- Miss N.Zvereva — 6/3 6/1
- Mrs P.Hy-Boulais — 7/6(2) 6/4
- Miss K.Kschwendt — 4/6 6/3 6/3
- Miss R.Dragomir — 6/7(7) 7/5 8/6
- Miss L.Courtois — 4/6 6/2 6/2
- Miss J.Novotna [6] — 6/4 6/0
- Miss C.Martinez [3] — 6/0 6/0
- Miss L.M.Raymond — 6/2 3/6 6/2
- Miss L.M.McNeil — 6/7(7) 6/4 6/4
- Miss K.Po — 6/4 6/3
- Miss K.Boogert — 5/7 6/4 6/2
- Miss K-A.Guse — 6/3 6/0
- Miss A-G.Sidot — 6/4 6/1
- Miss K.Date [12] — 6/0 6/3
- Miss M.Pierce [13] — 6/3 6/2
- Miss C.Taylor — 6/3 6/2
- Miss R.Hiraki — 7/5 6/4
- Miss N.Medvedeva — 5/7 7/5 6/4
- Miss E.Likhovtseva — 7/6(4) 6/3
- Miss K.M.Adams — 7/6(4) 6/1
- Mrs L.Neiland — 6/3 6/3
- Miss L.A.Davenport [8] — 6/4 6/1
- Mrs J.K.Wiesner — 6/0 7/5
- Miss M.Paz — 6/4 6/4
- Miss G.Pizzichini — 6/0 6/2
- Miss G.Fernandez — 2/6 6/3 6/4
- Miss S-H.Park — 6/2 6/2
- Miss A.Frazier — 6/3 6/1
- Miss I.Gorrochategui — 6/4 7/6(5)
- Miss I.Spirlea [15] — 3/6 6/1 6/2
- Mrs B.Schultz-McCarthy [11] — 6/0 6/2
- Miss J.Watanabe — 6/2 6/3
- Miss A.Olsza — 6/4 6/4
- Miss S.Appelmans — 6/3 6/4
- Miss F.Perfetti — 4/6 6/2 11/9
- Miss N.Sawamatsu — 7/6(3) 6/4
- Miss M.Oremans — 7/6(4) 6/3
- Miss A.Sanchez Vicario [4] — 6/3 6/4
- Miss A.Huber [5] — 6/1 6/1
- Miss P.H.Shriver — 6/4 6/4
- Miss H.Sukova — 6/3 6/3
- Miss A.Sugiyama — 7/5 6/4
- Miss B.Schett — 4/6 6/2 6/3
- Miss F.Labat — 6/1 2/6 7/5
- Miss S.Testud — 6/1 6/3
- Miss M.J.Fernandez [9] — 6/0 6/0
- Miss A.J.Coetzer [14] — 6/1 6/1
- Miss M.J.McGrath — 6/2 7/5
- Miss N.Feber — 6/1 6/1
- Miss A.Miller — 6/2 6/2
- Miss Y.Kamio — 6/2 6/3
- Mrs D.Van Roost — 6/3 6/3
- Miss K.Studenikova — 6/2 6/4
- Miss M.Seles [2] — 6/1 6/2

Third Round

- Miss S.Graf [1] — 7/5 6/3
- Miss N.J.Arendt — 2/6 6/2 6/3
- Miss L.M.Wild — 6/4 6/2
- Miss M.Hingis [16] — 6/1 6/1
- Miss N.Tauziat — 7/6(7) 3/6 9/7
- Mrs P.Hy-Boulais — 6/2 6/4
- Miss R.Dragomir — 6/2 6/0
- Miss J.Novotna [6] — 7/6(4) 6/3
- Miss C.Martinez [3] — 7/5 7/5
- Miss L.M.McNeil — 4/6 6/0 6/3
- Miss K.Boogert — 4/6 6/3 6/2
- Miss K.Date [12] — 6/7(5) 6/3 6/3
- Miss M.Pierce [13] — 6/4 6/2
- Miss N.Medvedeva — 6/3 6/2
- Miss E.Likhovtseva — 6/4 6/1
- Mrs L.Neiland — 6/3 6/2
- Mrs J.K.Wiesner — 6/2 6/3
- Miss G.Fernandez — 6/2 6/1
- Miss A.Frazier — 6/4 6/1
- Miss I.Gorrochategui — 6/3 2/6 6/4
- Mrs B.Schultz-McCarthy [11] — 6/3 6/0
- Miss S.Appelmans — 6/3 6/1
- Miss N.Sawamatsu — 6/4 6/0
- Miss A.Sanchez Vicario [4] — 7/5 6/3
- Miss A.Huber [5] — 6/2 6/1
- Miss A.Sugiyama — 6/4 6/1
- Miss F.Labat — 6/2 2/6 6/2
- Miss M.J.Fernandez [9] — 6/4 6/4
- Miss M.J.McGrath — 7/6(4) 2/6 6/3
- Miss N.Feber — 6/1 6/2
- Mrs D.Van Roost — 6/0 6/0
- Miss K.Studenikova — 7/5 5/7 6/4

Fourth Round

- Miss S.Graf [1] — 6/2 6/1
- Miss M.Hingis [16] — 6/3 2/6 6/1
- Miss J.Novotna [6] — 6/3 6/1
- Mrs P.Hy-Boulais — 6/3 3/6 6/4
- Miss C.Martinez [3] — 7/5 7/6(4)
- Miss K.Date [12] — 2/6 6/4 6/2
- Miss M.Pierce [13] — 6/4 6/1
- Miss E.Likhovtseva — 6/3 4/6 6/0
- Mrs J.K.Wiesner — 6/2 7/5
- Miss A.Frazier — 6/0 6/3
- Miss A.Sanchez Vicario [4] — 6/4 6/4
- Miss S.Appelmans — 7/5 3/6 12/10
- Miss A.Sugiyama — 7/6(3) 6/1
- Miss M.J.Fernandez [9] — 6/2 6/0
- Miss M.J.McGrath — 7/5 6/7(4) 6/2
- Miss K.Studenikova — 6/3 6/1

Quarter-Finals

- Miss S.Graf [1] — 6/1 6/4
- Miss J.Novotna [6] — 6/3 6/1
- Miss K.Date [12] — 5/7 7/6(5) 6/3
- Miss M.Pierce [13] — 6/2 6/3
- Mrs J.K.Wiesner — 6/4 6/4
- Miss A.Sanchez Vicario [4] — 3/6 6/2 6/1
- Miss M.J.Fernandez [9] — 6/4 1/6 6/3
- Miss M.J.McGrath — 6/4 6/0

Semi-Finals

- Miss S.Graf [1] — 6/3 6/2
- Miss K.Date [12] — 3/6 6/3 6/1
- Miss A.Sanchez Vicario [4] — 6/4 6/0
- Miss M.J.McGrath — 6/3 6/1

Final

- Miss S.Graf [1] — 6/2 2/6 6/3
- Miss A.Sanchez Vicario [4] — 6/2 6/1

Champion

- Miss S.Graf [1] — 6/3 7/5

Heavy type denotes seeded players. The figure in brackets against names denotes the order in which they have been seeded. (W) = Wild card. (Q) = Qualifier. (L) = Lucky loser.

The matches are the best of three sets

Holders: Miss J. Novotna and Miss A. Sanchez Vicario

The winners become the holders, for the year only, of the CHALLENGE CUP presented by HRH PRINCESS MARINA, DUCHESS OF KENT, the late President of The All England Lawn Tennis and Croquet Club. The winners receive silver replicas of the Challenge Cup. A silver salver is presented to each of the runners-up and a bronze medal to each defeated semi-finalist.

First Round

1. **Miss J.Novotna** (CZE) & **Miss A.Sanchez Vicario** (ESP) ....[1]
2. Miss A.Frazier (USA) & Miss K.Po (USA)
3. Miss R.Dragomir (ROM) & Miss A.Grossman (USA)
4. Miss S.Meier (GER) & Miss H.Nagyova (SVK)
(Q) 5. Miss I.Demongeot (FRA) & Miss C.Dhenin (FRA)
6. Miss L.Ghirardi (FRA) & Miss S.Pitkowski (FRA)
7. Miss A.Lettiere (USA) & Miss C.Morariu (USA)
8. **Miss K.Boogert** (NED) & **Miss I.Spirlea** (ROM) ....[11]
9. **Miss C.Martinez** (ESP) & **Miss P.Tarabini** (ARG) ....[13]
10. Miss K.Nagatsuka (JPN) & Miss A.Sugiyama (JPN)
11. Miss S.Farina (ITA) & Miss V.Ruano Pascual (ESP)
12. Miss R.Grande (ITA) & Miss E.Likhovtseva (RUS)
(W) 13. Miss S-A.Siddall (GBR) & Miss A.M.H.Wainwright (GBR)
14. Miss T.Krizan (SLO) & Miss C.Papadaki (GRE)
15. Miss C.G.Barclay (AUS) & Miss K.Godridge (AUS)
16. **Miss M.Hingis** (SUI) & **Miss H.Sukova** (CZE) ....[8]
17. **Miss L.A.Davenport** (USA) & **Miss M.J.Fernandez** (USA) [3]
18. Miss N.K.Kijimuta (JPN) & Miss Y.Yoshida (JPN)
19. Miss S.Jeyaseelan (CAN) & Miss R.Simpson (CAN)
20. Miss A.J.Coetzer (RSA) & Miss I.Gorrochategui (ARG)
21. Miss R.Bobkova (CZE) & Miss E.Melicharova (CZE)
22. Miss D.A.Graham (USA) & Miss M.Paz (ARG)
23. Miss W.Probst (GER) & Miss C.Singer (GER)
24. **Miss L.Golarsa** (ITA) & **Miss K.Radford** (AUS) ....[17]
25. **Miss P.D.Smylie** (AUS) & **Miss L.M.Wild** (USA) ....[15]
26. Miss K.Kschwendt (GER) & Miss F.Labat (ARG)
(L) 27. Miss D.J.Jones (AUS) & Miss T.A.Price (RSA)
28. Miss N.Dahlman (FIN) & Miss C.J.Wood (GBR)
29. Miss L.Montalvo (ARG) & Miss P.Suarez (ARG)
30. Miss N.Miyagi (JPN) & Miss S.Reece (USA)
31. Miss O.Lugina (UKR) & Mrs E.Wagner (GER)
32. **Miss L.M.Raymond** (USA) & **Miss R.P.Stubbs** (AUS) ....[9]
33. **Miss L.M.McNeil** (USA) & **Miss N.Tauziat** (FRA) ....[7]
34. Miss N.Feber (BEL) & Mrs D.Van Roost (BEL)
(W) 35. Miss B.Nagelsen (USA) & Miss M.Seles (USA)
36. Mrs R.Nideffer (RSA) & Miss P.H.Shriver (USA)
37. Mrs M.Werdel Witmeyer (USA) & Miss T.S.Whitlinger-Jones (USA)
38. Miss M.Grzybowska (POL) & Miss A.Olsza (POL)
39. Miss E.S.H.Callens (BEL) & Miss L.Courtois (BEL)
40. **Miss K.M.Adams** (USA) & **Miss M.de Swardt** (RSA) ....[10]
41. **Mrs A.Dechaume-Balleret** (FRA) & **Miss S.Testud** (FRA) ..[14]
42. Miss E.R.De Lone (USA) & Miss N.J.Pratt (AUS)
43. Miss M.Koutstaal (NED) & Miss S-H.Park (KOR)
44. Miss S.Appelmans (BEL) & Miss M.Oremans (NED)
45. Miss R.Hiraki (JPN) & Mrs P.Hy-Boulais (CAN)
46. Miss D.Krajcovicova (SVK) & Miss R.Zrubakova (SVK)
(W) 47. Miss H.Crook (GBR) & Miss V.Davies (GBR)
48. **Miss M.J.McGrath** (USA) & **Mrs L.Neiland** (LAT) ....[4]
49. **Miss N.J.Arendt** (USA) & **Miss M.M.Bollegraf** (NED) ......[6]
50. Miss A-M.Cecchini (ITA) & Miss L.Garrone (ITA)
51. Miss A.Carlsson (SWE) & Miss A.Temesvari (HUN)
52. Miss C.Cristea (ROM) & Miss C.Schneider (GER)
(L) 53. Miss J.Lutrova (RUS) & Miss T.Tanasugarn (THA)
54. Miss M.Lindstrom (SWE) & Miss M.Strandlund (SWE)
(Q) 55. Miss J.M.Pullin (GBR) & Miss L.A.Woodroffe (GBR)
56. **Miss Y.Basuki** (INA) & **Miss C.M.Vis** (NED) ....[12]
57. **Mrs N.Bradtke** (AUS) & **Miss R.McQuillan** (AUS) ....[16]
(W) 58. Miss V.Lake (GBR) & Miss S.Smith (GBR)
59. Miss M.Muric (CRO) & Miss K.Studenikova (SVK)
60. Miss J.M.Hetherington (CAN) & Mrs K.S.Rinaldi-Stunkel (USA)
61. Miss T.Jecmenica (YUG) & Miss C.Porwik (GER)
62. Miss A.Fusai (FRA) & Miss K-A.Guse (AUS)
63. Miss P.Langrova (CZE) & Miss H.Vildova (CZE)
64. **Miss G.Fernandez** (USA) & **Miss N.Zvereva** (BLR) ....[2]

Second Round

Miss J.Novotna & Miss A.Sanchez Vicario [1] — 4/6 6/2 6/1
Miss R.Dragomir & Miss A.Grossman — 6/2 7/6(3)
Miss I.Demongeot & Miss C.Dhenin — 6/3 6/0
Miss K.Boogert & Miss I.Spirlea [11] — 7/6(4) 6/1
Miss C.Martinez & Miss P.Tarabini [13] — 7/5 6/3
Miss R.Grande & Miss E.Likhovtseva — 6/3 6/2
Miss T.Krizan & Miss C.Papadaki — 4/6 6/3 6/2
Miss M.Hingis & Miss H.Sukova [8] — 6/1 7/5
Miss L.A.Davenport & Miss M.J.Fernandez [3] — 6/3 1/6 6/1
Miss A.J.Coetzer & Miss I.Gorrochategui — 5/7 6/2 6/1
Miss D.A.Graham & Miss M.Paz — 5/7 6/4 6/2
Miss W.Probst & Miss C.Singer — 4/6 6/4 6/2
Mrs P.D.Smylie & Miss L.M.Wild [15] — 6/2 6/1
Miss D.J.Jones & Miss T.A.Price — 6/4 6/4
Miss N.Miyagi & Miss S.Reece — 6/4 6/4
Miss L.M.Raymond & Miss R.P.Stubbs [9] — 6/4 6/4
Miss L.M.McNeil & Miss N.Tauziat [7] — 7/6(3) 1/6 6/4
Mrs R.Nideffer & Miss P.H.Shriver — 4/6 6/4 9/7
Mrs M.Werdel Witmeyer & Mrs T.S.Whitlinger-Jones — 6/4 6/1
Miss K.M.Adams & Miss M.de Swardt [10] — 6/1 6/4
Mrs A.Dechaume-Balleret & Miss S.Testud [14] — 6/3 6/2
Miss S.Appelmans & Miss M.Oremans — 6/4 6/2
Miss R.Hiraki & Mrs P.Hy-Boulais — 6/3 6/4
Miss M.J.McGrath & Mrs L.Neiland [4] — 6/2 6/4
Miss N.J.Arendt & Miss M.M.Bollegraf [6] — 6/3 7/5
Miss A.Carlsson & Miss A.Temesvari — 6/0 6/4
Miss J.Lutrova & Miss T.Tanasugarn — 7/6(4) 6/4
Miss Y.Basuki & Miss C.M.Vis [12] — 6/3 6/0
Mrs N.Bradtke & Miss R.McQuillan [16] — 6/2 6/3
Miss J.M.Hetherington & Mrs K.S.Rinaldi-Stunkel — 6/4 6/2
Miss A.Fusai & Miss K-A.Guse — 6/3 6/7(7) 6/4
Miss G.Fernandez & Miss N.Zvereva [2] — 6/2 6/1

Third Round

Miss J.Novotna & Miss A.Sanchez Vicario [1] — 6/0 6/1
Miss K.Boogert & Miss I.Spirlea [11] — 6/4 6/2
Miss C.Martinez & Miss P.Tarabini [13] — 7/6(2) 6/4
Miss M.Hingis & Miss H.Sukova [8] — 6/4 6/3
Miss L.A.Davenport & Miss M.J.Fernandez [3] — 6/3 6/2
Miss W.Probst & Miss C.Singer — 6/3 6/2
Mrs P.D.Smylie & Miss L.M.Wild [15] — 6/4 6/4
Miss L.M.Raymond & Miss R.P.Stubbs [9] — 7/5 6/4
Mrs R.Nideffer & Miss P.H.Shriver — 6/7(5) 6/4 6/1
Miss K.M.Adams & Miss M.de Swardt [10] — 6/7(4) 6/2 6/2
Mrs A.Dechaume-Balleret & Miss S.Testud [14] — 7/6(6) 6/4
Miss M.J.McGrath & Mrs L.Neiland [4] — 6/2 6/4
Miss N.J.Arendt & Miss M.M.Bollegraf [6] — 6/1 6/4
Miss Y.Basuki & Miss C.M.Vis [12] — 7/6(3) 6/7(4) 6/4
Mrs N.Bradtke & Miss R.McQuillan [16] — 6/3 6/1
Miss G.Fernandez & Miss N.Zvereva [2] — 6/3 6/2

Fourth Round

Miss J.Novotna & Miss A.Sanchez Vicario [1] — 6/3 6/3
Miss M.Hingis & Miss H.Sukova [8] — 7/6(5) 6/0
Miss L.A.Davenport & Miss M.J.Fernandez [3] — 6/2 6/2
Mrs P.D.Smylie & Miss L.M.Wild [15] — 6/4 7/5
Miss K.M.Adams & Miss M.de Swardt [10] — 6/1 6/4
Miss M.J.McGrath & Mrs L.Neiland [4] — 6/3 RTD
Miss Y.Basuki & Miss C.M.Vis [12] — 6/2 7/6(3)
Miss G.Fernandez & Miss N.Zvereva [2] — 6/2 6/1

Quarter-finals

Miss M.Hingis & Miss H.Sukova [8] — 3/6 7/6(4) 6/3
Mrs P.D.Smylie & Miss L.M.Wild [15] — 5/3 Ret'd.
Miss M.J.McGrath & Mrs L.Neiland [4] — 6/3 RTD
Miss G.Fernandez & Miss N.Zvereva [2]

Semi-finals

Miss M.Hingis & Miss H.Sukova [8] — 6/4 4/6 6/4
Miss M.J.McGrath & Mrs L.Neiland [4] — 6/4 3/6 11/9

Final

Miss M.Hingis & Miss H.Sukova [8] — 5/7 7/5 6/1

Heavy type denotes seeded players. The figure in brackets against names denotes the order in which they have been seeded.
(W) = Wild card. (Q) = Qualifier. (L) = Lucky loser.

The matches are the best of three sets

Holders: J. Stark and Miss M. Navratilova

First Round	Second Round	Third Round	Quarter-Finals	Semi-Finals	Final
1. M.Woodforde (AUS) & Mrs L.Neiland (LAT) [1]	M.Woodforde & Mrs L.Neiland [1]				
2. B.Haygarth (RSA) & Miss C.Singer (GER)	6/4 3/6 10/8	M.Woodforde & Mrs L.Neiland [1]			
3. K.Flach (USA) & Miss R.Nideffer (RSA)	K.Flach & Mrs R.Nideffer		w/o		
4. P.Norval (RSA) & Miss C.Papadaki (GRE)	6/3 7/6(5)	M.J.Bates & Mrs N.Bradtke	M.Woodforde & Mrs L.Neiland [1]		
(W) 5. M.J.Bates (GBR) & Mrs N.Bradtke (AUS)	M.J.Bates & Mrs N.Bradtke		6/4 6/4		
6. G.Koves (HUN) & Miss A.Temesvari (HUN)	6/1 6/3				
7. M.Huning (GER) & Miss D.A.Graham (USA)	J.Grabb & Miss L.M.Wild [13]	M.J.Bates & Mrs N.Bradtke			
8. J.Grabb (USA) & Miss L.M.Wild (USA) [13]	7/5 7/6(9)	6/7(3) 6/3 6/0			
9. J.A.Conde (ESP) & Miss V.Ruano Pascual (ESP)	J.Eagle & A.Ellwood			M.Woodforde & Mrs L.Neiland [1]	
10. J.Eagle (AUS) & Miss A.Ellwood (AUS)	3/6 6/4 7/5	J.Eagle & Miss A.Ellwood		3/6 6/2 7/5	
11. S.E.Davis (USA) & Miss P.Tarabini (ARG)	S.E.Davis & Miss P.Tarabini		7/6(1) 6/2		
12. G.Van Emburgh (USA) & Miss I.Spirlea (ROM)	6/3 4/6 6/3	J.Eagle & Miss A.Ellwood			
13. B.MacPhie (USA) & Mrs T.S.Whitlinger-Jones (USA)	B.MacPhie & Mrs T.S.Whitlinger-Jones				
14. S.Cannon (USA) & Mrs P.Hy-Boulais (CAN)	7/6(6) 6/1	P.Galbraith & Miss P.H.Shriver [8]			
15. M.Tebbutt (AUS) & Miss K.Radford (AUS)	P.Galbraith & Miss P.H.Shriver [8]		6/4 6/4		
16. P.Galbraith (USA) & Miss P.H.Shriver (USA) [8]	7/6(2) 6/3	6/4 6/4	P.Galbraith & Miss P.H.Shriver [8]		
17. M.Knowles (BAH) & Miss L.M.Raymond (USA) [3]	R.Bergh & Miss K.Po		6/2 6/4		
18. R.Bergh (SWE) & Miss K.Po (USA)	6/4 3/6 6/3	R.Bergh & Miss K.Po			
19. W.Arthurs (AUS) & Miss K.Godridge (AUS)	D.Adams & Miss K-A.Guse		7/5 7/6(4)		
20. D.Adams (RSA) & Miss K-A.Guse (AUS)	7/6(2) 6/7(5) 6/4	R.Bergh & Miss K.Po		M.Woodforde & Mrs L.Neiland [1]	
21. M.Oosting (NED) & Miss E.S.H.Callens (BEL)	M.Oosting & Miss E.S.H.Callens		6/3 6/4	6/3 3/6 6/2	
22. L.J.Bale (RSA) & Miss Y.Basuki (INA)	6/4 6/4	P.Cash & Miss M.Pierce			
(W) 23. P.Cash (AUS) & Miss M.Pierce (FRA)	P.Cash & Miss M.Pierce		6/2 5/7 8/6		
24. L.Pimek (BEL) & Miss K.M.Adams (USA) [11]	6/4 6/3		R.Bergh & Miss K.Po		
25. E.Ferreira (RSA) & Miss M.de Swardt (RSA) [9]	C.J.Van Rensburg & Miss L.Golarsa			C.J.Van Rensburg & Miss L.Golarsa	
26. C.J.Van Rensburg (RSA) & Miss L.Golarsa (ITA)	6/4 6/4	C.J.Van Rensburg & Miss L.Golarsa		6/4 6/4	
27. J-L.De Jager (RSA) & Miss J.M.Hetherington (CAN)	L.Manta & Miss M.Hingis		6/4 6/4		
28. L.Manta (SUI) & Miss M.Hingis (SUI)	6/3 6/3		C.J.Van Rensburg & Miss L.Golarsa		
29. S.Schalken (NED) & Miss E.R.De Lone (USA)	D.E.Sapsford & Miss S-A.Siddall		7/6(5) 6/3		
(W) 30. D.E.Sapsford (GBR) & Miss S-A.Siddall (GBR)	6/3 6/7(4) 6/3	D.E.Sapsford & Miss S-A.Siddall			
31. T.Nijssen (NED) & Miss C.Porwik (GER)	T.Nijssen & Miss C.Porwik		6/4 6/7(2) 6/4		
32. P.T.Hand (GBR) & Miss V.Lake (GBR)	6/2 6/2			C.Suk & Miss H.Sukova [7]	
33. C.Suk (CZE) & Miss H.Sukova (CZE) [7]	C.Suk & Miss H.Sukova [7]			1/6 6/3 6/2	
34. F.Montana (USA) & Miss L.Pleming (USA)	6/3 6/2	C.Suk & Miss H.Sukova [7]			
35. P.Tramacchi (AUS) & Miss R.P.Stubbs (AUS)	P.Tramacchi & Miss R.P.Stubbs		5/7 7/6(3) 6/2		
36. S.Noteboom (NED) & Miss M.Paz (ARG)	6/4 6/4	C.Suk & Miss H.Sukova [7]			
37. D.Macpherson (AUS) & Miss R.McQuillan (AUS)	D.Macpherson & Miss R.McQuillan		6/1 4/6 6/3		
38. N.Broad (GBR) & Miss A.Grossman (USA)	6/4 7/5	D.Macpherson & Miss R.McQuillan			
39. M.Lucena (USA) & Miss M.J.McGrath (USA)	M.Lucena & Miss M.J.McGrath		W/O		
40. B.Talbot (RSA) & Miss C.M.Vis (NED) [14]	6/3 4/6 6/4		C.Suk & Miss H.Sukova [7]		
(W) 41. H.Guenthardt (SUI) & Miss S.Graf (GER) [15]	H.Guenthardt & Miss S.Graf [15]		6/3 2/6 10/8	C.Suk & Miss H.Sukova [7]	
42. A.Florent (AUS) & Miss C.G.Barclay (AUS)	6/1 7/5	S.Draper & Mrs P.D.Smylie		6/4 6/2	
43. S.Draper (AUS) & Mrs P.D.Smylie (AUS)	S.Draper & Mrs P.D.Smylie		w/o		
44. L.Paes (IND) & Miss K.Nagatsuka (JPN)	6/4 6/4	L.B.Jensen & Miss N.J.Arendt			
45. L.B.Jensen (USA) & Miss N.J.Arendt (USA)	L.B.Jensen & Miss N.J.Arendt		6/7(7) 7/5 6/4		
46. P.Kilderry (AUS) & Miss A.Sugiyama (JPN)	6/4 7/6(1)	L.B.Jensen & Miss N.J.Arendt			
47. H.J.Davids (NED) & Miss M.Oremans (NED)	H.J.Davids & Miss M.Oremans		7/6(5) 6/2		
48. R.Leach (USA) & Miss M.M.Bollegraf (NED) [4]	6/3 6/3			C.Suk & Miss H.Sukova [7]	
(W) 49. J.Stark (USA) & Miss M.Navratilova (USA) [5]	J.Stark & Miss M.Navratilova [5]			6/4 6/2	
50. A.Kratzmann (AUS) & Miss M.Lindstrom (SWE)	6/3 3/6 6/2	J.Stark & Miss M.Navratilova [5]			
51. J.Belloli (USA) & Miss I.Montalvo (ARG)	K.Kinnear & Miss N.Miyagi		7/5 7/6(3)		
52. K.Kinnear (USA) & Miss N.Miyagi (JPN)	6/3 6/3	J.Stark & Miss M.Navratilova [5]			
53. M.Barnard (RSA) & Miss S.Reece (USA)	M.Ondruska & Miss K.Kschwendt		7/6(2) 6/7(4) 7/5		
54. M.Ondruska (RSA) & Miss K.Kschwendt (GER)	7/6(4) 6/7(4) 6/3	M.Ondruska & Miss K.Kschwendt			
55. J.Ireland (AUS) & Miss P.Suarez (ARG)	A.Olhovskiy & Miss K.Boogert [10]		2/6 6/2 7/5		
56. A.Olhovskiy (RUS) & Miss K.Boogert (NED) [10]	6/3 6/2		J.Stark & Miss M.Navratilova [5]		
57. M.Keil (USA) & Miss L.M.McNeil (USA) [12]	M.Keil & Miss L.M.McNeil [12]		6/4 7/6(4)	G.Connell & Miss L.A.Davenport [2]	
58. K.Jones (USA) & Mrs K.S.Rinaldi-Stunkel (USA)	6/4 7/5	M.Keil & Miss L.M.McNeil [12]		7/6(5) 7/6(2)	
59. P.Nyborg (SWE) & Miss M.Strandlund (SWE)	P.Nyborg & Miss M.Strandlund		6/4 7/6(4)		
60. M.R.J.Petchey (GBR) & Miss C.J.Wood (GBR)	6/4 2/6 8/6	G.Connell & Miss L.A.Davenport [2]			
61. T.Kempers (NED) & Miss A.Olsza (POL)	T.Kempers & Miss A.Olsza		6/4 6/0		
62. J.Waite (USA) & Miss N.Feber (BEL)	7/6(1) 6/3	G.Connell & Miss L.A.Davenport [2]			
63. K.Thorne (USA) & Miss A.Fusai (FRA)	G.Connell & Miss L.A.Davenport [2]		6/2 6/3		
64. G.Connell (CAN) & Miss L.A.Davenport (USA) [2]	2/6 6/2 16/14				

Winner: **M.Woodforde & Mrs L.Neiland [1]** — 6/3 3/6 6/2

THE 35 AND OVER GENTLEMEN'S INVITATION DOUBLES

Holders: P. B. McNamara and L. Shiras

The winners become the holders, for the year only, of a Cup presented by The All England Lawn Tennis and Croquet Club. The winners receive miniature silver salvers. A silver medal is presented to each of the runners-up.

GROUP A

Pair		Opponents & scores			WINS	LOSSES
S.Glickstein (ISR) and P.F.McNamee (AUS)	v	A.M.Jarrett (GBR) and J.R.Smith (GBR) 7/6(4) 7/6(5)	P.Slozil (CZE) and T.Smid (CZE) w/o to Slozil and Smid	A.A.Mayer (USA) and G.Mayer (USA) 6/4 1/1 Ret'd.	1	2
A.M.Jarrett (GBR) and J.R.Smith (GBR)	v	**S.Glickstein (ISR) and P.F.McNamee (AUS)** 6/7(4) 6/7(5)	P.Slozil (CZE) and T.Smid (CZE) 6/4 3/6 12/10	A.A.Mayer (USA) and G.Mayer (USA) 3/6 2/6	1	2
A.A.Mayer (USA) and G.Mayer (USA)	v	P.Slozil (CZE) and T.Smid (CZE) 3/6 3/6	**S.Glickstein (ISR) and P.F.McNamee (AUS)** 4/6 1/1 Ret'd.	A.M.Jarrett (GBR) and J.R.Smith (GBR) 6/3 6/2	2	1
P.Slozil (CZE) and T.Smid (CZE)	v	A.A.Mayer (USA) and G.Mayer (USA) 6/3 6/3	A.M.Jarrett (GBR) and J.R.Smith (GBR) 4/6 6/3 10/12	**S.Glickstein (ISR) and P.F.McNamee (AUS)** w/o to Slozil and Smid	2	1

GROUP B

Pair		Opponents & scores			WINS	LOSSES
A.Amritraj (IND) and V.Amritraj (IND)	v	R.L.Case (AUS) and R.J.Frawley (AUS) 6/2 6/3	H.Guenthardt (SUI) and B.Taroczy (HUN) 4/6 6/4 6/3	J.B.Fitzgerald (AUS) and R.Tanner (USA) 4/6 1/6	2	1
R.L.Case (AUS) and R.J.Frawley (AUS)	v	**A.Amritraj (IND) and V.Amritraj (IND)** 2/6 3/6	J.B.Fitzgerald (AUS) and R.Tanner (USA) 4/6 3/6	H.Guenthardt (SUI) and B.Taroczy (HUN) 6/3 3/6 4/6	0	3
H.Guenthardt (SUI) and B.Taroczy (HUN)	v	J.B.Fitzgerald (AUS) and R.Tanner (USA) 6/7(14) 2/6	**A.Amritraj (IND) and V.Amritraj (IND)** 6/4 4/6 3/6	R.L.Case (AUS) and R.J.Frawley (AUS) 3/6 6/3 6/4	1	2
J.B.Fitzgerald (AUS) and R.Tanner (USA)	v	H.Guenthardt (SUI) and B.Taroczy (HUN) 7/6(14) 6/2	R.L.Case (AUS) and R.J.Frawley (AUS) 6/4 6/3	**A.Amritraj (IND) and V.Amritraj (IND)** 6/4 6/1	3	0

GROUP C

Pair		Opponents & scores			WINS	LOSSES
B.E.Gottfried (USA) and R.Ramirez (MEX)	v	C.Dowdeswell (GBR) and C.J.Mottram (GBR) 6/7(4) 7/5 4/6	M.R.Edmondson (AUS) and K.Warwick (AUS) 1/6 2/6	K.Curren (USA) and J.C.Kriek (USA) 5/7 4/6	0	3
C.Dowdeswell (GBR) and C.J.Mottram (GBR)	v	**B.E.Gottfried (USA) and R.Ramirez (MEX)** 7/6(4) 5/7 6/4	M.R.Edmondson (AUS) and K.Warwick (AUS) 6/4 3/6 12/10	K.Curren (USA) and J.C.Kriek (USA) 2/6 7/6(3) 4/6	2	1
M.R.Edmondson (AUS) and K.Warwick (AUS)	v	K.Curren (USA) and J.C.Kriek (USA) 7/5 7/6(5)	**B.E.Gottfried (USA) and R.Ramirez (MEX)** 6/1 6/2	C.Dowdeswell (GBR) and C.J.Mottram (GBR) 4/6 6/3 10/12	2	1
K.Curren (USA) and J.C.Kriek (USA)	v	M.R.Edmondson (AUS) and K.Warwick (AUS) 5/7 6/7(5)	**B.E.Gottfried (USA) and R.Ramirez (MEX)** 7/5 6/4	C.Dowdeswell (GBR) and C.J.Mottram (GBR) 6/2 6/7(3) 6/4	2	1

GROUP D

Pair		Opponents & scores			WINS	LOSSES
M.Bahrami (IRN) and J.Higueras (ESP)	v	W.Fibak (POL) and T.Wilkison (USA) 3/6 3/6	T.R.Gullikson (USA) and L.Shiras (USA) 3/6 2/6	P.Fleming (USA) and H.Pfister (USA) 1/6 4/6	0	3
W.Fibak (POL) and T.Wilkison (USA)	v	**M.Bahrami (IRN) and J.Higueras (ESP)** 6/3 6/3	T.R.Gullikson (USA) and L.Shiras (USA) 6/3 7/5	P.Fleming (USA) and H.Pfister (USA) 6/4 6/4	3	0
P.Fleming (USA) and H.Pfister (USA)	v	T.R.Gullikson (USA) and L.Shiras (USA) 7/6(3) 6/7(4) 6/3	**M.Bahrami (IRN) and J.Higueras (ESP)** 6/1 6/4	W.Fibak (POL) and T.Wilkison (USA) 4/6 4/6	2	1
T.R.Gullikson (USA) and L.Shiras (USA)	v	P.Fleming (USA) and H.Pfister (USA) 6/7(3) 7/6(4) 3/6	**M.Bahrami (IRN) and J.Higueras (ESP)** 6/3 6/2	W.Fibak (POL) and T.Wilkison (USA) 3/6 5/7	1	2

SEMI-FINAL

P.Slozil (CZE) and T.Smid (CZE)
J.B.Fitzgerald (AUS) and R.Tanner (USA)
— P.Slozil (CZE) and T.Smid (CZE) 6/3 7/5

M.R.Edmondson (AUS) and K.Warwick (AUS)
W.Fibak (POL) and T.Wilkison (USA)
— W.Fibak (POL) and T.Wilkison (USA) 7/6(4) 6/7(4) 6/4

FINAL

W.Fibak (POL) and T.Wilkison (USA) 6/2 5/7 6/1

This event is played on a 'round robin' basis. Sixteen invited pairs are divided into four groups and each pair in each group plays the others. The pairs winning most matches are the winners of their respective groups and play semi-final and final rounds as indicated above.
If matches should be equal in any group, the head-to-head result between the two pairs with the same number of wins determines the winning pair of the group.

Heavy type denotes seeded players.

The matches are the best of three sets

Holders: Miss W. M. Turnbull and Miss S. V. Wade

GROUP A			RESULTS		FINAL
			WINS	LOSSES	
Miss W.M.Turnbull (AUS) and Miss S.V.Wade (GBR)	v	Miss R.Casals (USA) and Miss B.F.Stove (NED) 6/3 6/2 / Miss M.Jausovec (SLO) and Miss Y.Vermaak (RSA) 6/1 2/6 7/9	1	1	
Miss R.Casals (USA) and Miss B.F.Stove (NED)	v	Miss W.M.Turnbull (AUS) and Miss S.V.Wade (GBR) 3/6 2/6 / Miss M.Jausovec (SLO) and Miss Y.Vermaak (RSA) 0/6 5/7	0	2	Miss M.Jausovec (SLO) and Miss Y.Vermaak (RSA)
Miss M.Jausovec (SLO) and Miss Y.Vermaak (RSA)	v	Miss W.M.Turnbull (AUS) and Miss S.V.Wade (GBR) 1/6 6/2 9/7 / Miss R.Casals (USA) and Miss B.F.Stove (NED) 6/0 7/5	2	0	
GROUP B					Miss J.M.Durie (GBR) and Miss A.E.Smith (USA) 6/3 6/2
Miss B.Nagelsen (USA) and Miss J.C.Russell (USA)	v	Miss J.M.Durie (GBR) and Miss A.E.Smith (USA) 3/6 7/5 1/6 / Miss H.Gourlay (AUS) and Mrs G.E.Reid (AUS) w/o to Gourlay and Reid	0	2	
Miss J.M.Durie (GBR) and Miss A.E.Smith (USA)	v	Miss B.Nagelsen (USA) and Miss J.C.Russell (USA) 6/3 5/7 6/1 / Miss H.Gourlay (AUS) and Mrs G.E.Reid (AUS) 6/1 6/3	2	0	Miss J.M.Durie (GBR) and Miss A.E.Smith (USA)
Miss H.Gourlay (AUS) and Mrs G.E.Reid (AUS)	v	Miss B.Nagelsen (USA) and Miss J.C.Russell (USA) w/o to Gourlay and Reid / Miss J.M.Durie (GBR) and Miss A.E.Smith (USA) 1/6 3/6	1	1	

This event is played on a 'round robin' basis.Six invited pairs are divided into two groups and each pair in each group plays the others. The pairs winning most matches are the winners of their respective groups and play a final round as indicated above. If matches should be equal in any group, the head-to-head result between the two pairs with the same number of wins determines the winning pair of the group.

Heavy type denotes seeded players.
The matches are the best of three sets

ALPHABETICAL LIST – 35 & OVER EVENTS

GENTLEMEN'S

Amritraj A. *(India)*
Amritraj V. *(India)*
Bahrami M. *(Iran)*
Case R.L. *(Australia)*
Curren K. *(USA)*
Dowdeswell C. *(Great Britain)*
Edmondson M.R. *(Australia)*
Fibak W.J. *(Poland)*

Fitzgerald J.B. *(Australia)*
Fleming P. *(USA)*
Frawley R.J. *(Australia)*
Glickstein S. *(Israel)*
Gottfried B.E. *(USA)*
Guenthardt H. *(Switzerland)*
Gullikson T.R. *(USA)*
Higueras J. *(Spain)*

Jarrett A.M. *(Great Britain)*
Kriek J.C. *(USA)*
Mayer G. *(USA)*
Mayer A.A. *(USA)*
McNamee P.F. *(Australia)*
Mottram C.J. *(Great Britain)*
Pfister H. *(USA)*
Ramirez R. *(Mexico)*

Shiras L. *(USA)*
Slozil P. *(Czech Republic)*
Smid T. *(Czech Republic)*
Smith J.R. *(Great Britain)*
Tanner R. *(USA)*
Taroczy B. *(Hungary)*
Warwick K. *(Australia)*
Wilkison T. *(USA)*

LADIES'

Casals Miss R. *(USA)*
Durie Miss J.M. *(Great Britain)*
Gourlay Miss H. *(Australia)*

Jausovec Miss M. *(Slovenia)*
Nagelsen Miss B. *(USA)*
Reid Mrs G.E. *(Australia)*

Russell Miss J.C. *(USA)*
Smith Miss A.E. *(USA)*
Stove Miss B.F. *(Netherlands)*

Turnbull Miss W.M. *(Australia)*
Vermaak Miss Y. *(South Africa)*
Wade Miss S.V. *(Great Britain)*

ALPHABETICAL LIST – 45 & OVER EVENT

GENTLEMEN'S

Alexander J.G. *(Australia)*
Battrick G. *(Great Britain)*
Cox M. *(Great Britain)*
Davidson O.K. *(Australia)*
Dent P.C. *(Australia)*
Drysdale E.C. *(South Africa)*

Fraser N.A. *(Australia)*
Hewitt R.A.J. *(South Africa)*
Kodes J. *(Czech Republic)*
Masters G. *(Australia)*
McMillan F.D. *(South Africa)*
Metreveli A. *(Russia)*

Nastase I. *(Romania)*
Newcombe J.D. *(Australia)*
Okker T.S. *(Netherlands)*
Riessen M.C. *(USA)*
Roche A.D. *(Australia)*
Rosewall K.R. *(Australia)*

Santana M. *(Spain)*
Smith S.R. *(USA)*
Stewart S.E. *(USA)*
Stolle F.S. *(Australia)*
Stone A.J. *(Australia)*
Taylor R. *(Great Britain)*

For both the Boys' Singles *and* the Boys' Doubles Championships, the winners become the holders, for the year only, of a Cup presented by The All England Lawn Tennis and Croquet Club. The winners each receive a miniature Cup and the runners-up receive mementoes.

Holder: O. Mutis

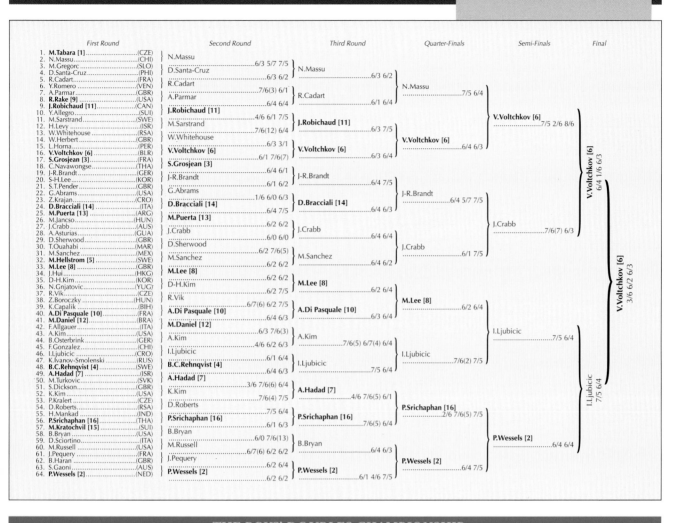

First Round	Second Round	Third Round	Quarter-Finals	Semi-Finals	Final
1. **M.Tabara [1]** (CZE)					
2. N.Massu (CHI)	N.Massu 6/3 5/7 7/5				
3. M.Gregorc (SLO)		N.Massu			
4. D.Santa-Cruz (PHI)	D.Santa-Cruz 6/3 6/2	6/3 6/2			
5. R.Cadart (FRA)			N.Massu		
6. Y.Romero (VEN)	R.Cadart 7/6(3) 6/1				
7. A.Parmar (GBR)		R.Cadart			
8. **R.Rake [9]** (USA)	A.Parmar	6/1 6/4			
9. **J.Robichaud [11]** (CAN)	**J.Robichaud [11]**			7/5 6/4	
10. Y.Allegro (SUI)	4/6 6/1 7/5				
11. M.Sarstrand (SWE)		**J.Robichaud [11]**			
12. H.Levy (ISR)	M.Sarstrand 7/6(12) 6/4	6/3 7/5			
13. W.Whitehouse (RSA)			**V.Voltchkov [6]**		
14. W.Herbert (GBR)	W.Whitehouse 6/3 3/1		6/4 6/3		
15. L.Horna (PER)		**V.Voltchkov [6]**			
16. **V.Voltchkov [6]** (BLR)	**V.Voltchkov [6]** 6/1 7/6(7)	6/3 6/4		**V.Voltchkov [6]**	
17. **S.Grosjean [3]** (FRA)	**S.Grosjean [3]**			7/5 2/6 8/6	
18. C.Navawongse (THA)	6/4 6/1				
19. J-R.Brandt (GER)	J-R.Brandt	J-R.Brandt			
20. S-H.Lee (KOR)	6/1 6/2	6/4 7/5			
21. S.T.Pender (GBR)	G.Abrams		J-R.Brandt		
22. G.Abrams (USA)	1/6 6/0 6/3		6/4 5/7 7/5		
23. Z.Krajan (CRO)	**D.Bracciali [14]**	**D.Bracciali [14]**			
24. **D.Bracciali [14]** (ITA)	6/4 7/5	6/4 6/3			
25. **M.Puerta [13]** (ARG)	**M.Puerta [13]**			J.Crabb	
26. M.Jancso (HUN)	6/2 6/2			7/6(7) 6/3	
27. J.Crabb (AUS)	J.Crabb	J.Crabb			
28. A.Asturias (GUA)	6/0 6/0	6/4 6/4			
29. D.Sherwood (GBR)	D.Sherwood		J.Crabb		
30. T.Ouahabi (MAR)	6/2 7/6(5)		6/1 7/5		
31. M.Sanchez (MEX)	M.Sanchez	M.Sanchez			
32. **M.Hellstrom [5]** (SWE)	6/2 6/2	6/4 6/2			
33. **M.Lee [8]** (GBR)	**M.Lee [8]**				
34. J.Hui (HKG)	6/2 6/0				
35. D-H.Kim (KOR)	D-H.Kim	**M.Lee [8]**			
36. M.Gnjatovic (YUG)	6/2 7/5	6/2 6/4			
37. R.Vik (CZE)	R.Vik		**M.Lee [8]**		
38. Z.Boroczky (HUN)	6/7(6) 6/2 7/6		6/2 6/4		
39. K.Capalik (BIH)	**A.Di Pasquale [10]**	**A.Di Pasquale [10]**			
40. **A.Di Pasquale [10]** (FRA)	6/4 6/3	6/3 6/4			
41. **M.Daniel [12]** (BRA)	**M.Daniel [12]**			I.Ljubicic	
42. F.Allgauer (ITA)	6/3 7/6(3)			7/5 6/4	
43. A.Kim (USA)	A.Kim	A.Kim			
44. B.Osterbrink (GER)	4/6 6/2 6/3	7/6(5) 6/7(4) 6/4			
45. F.Gonzalez (CHI)	I.Ljubicic		I.Ljubicic		
46. I.Ljubicic (CRO)	6/1 6/4		7/6(2) 7/5		
47. K.Ivanov-Smolenski (RUS)	**B.C.Rehnqvist [4]**	I.Ljubicic			
48. **B.C.Rehnqvist [4]** (SWE)		7/5 6/4			I.Ljubicic
49. **A.Hadad [7]** (ISR)	**A.Hadad [7]**				7/5 6/4
50. M.Turkovic (SVK)	3/6 7/6(6) 6/4				
51. S.Dickson (GBR)	K.Kim	**A.Hadad [7]**			
52. K.Kim (USA)	7/6(4) 7/5	4/6 7/6(5) 6/1			
53. P.Kralert (CZE)	D.Roberts		**P.Srichaphan [16]**		
54. D.Roberts (RSA)	7/5 6/4		2/6 7/6(5) 7/5		
55. H.Mankad (IND)	**P.Srichaphan [16]**	**P.Srichaphan [16]**			
56. **P.Srichaphan [16]** (THA)	6/1 6/3	7/6(5) 6/4			
57. **M.Kratochvil [15]** (SUI)	B.Bryan			**P.Wessels [2]**	
58. B.Bryan (USA)	6/0 7/6(13)			6/4 6/4	
59. D.Sciortino (ITA)	M.Russell	B.Bryan			
60. M.Russell (USA)	6/7(6) 6/4 6/2	6/4 6/3			
61. J.Pequery (FRA)	J.Pequery		**P.Wessels [2]**		
62. B.Haran (GBR)	6/2 6/4		6/4 7/5		
63. S.Gaoni (AUS)	**P.Wessels [2]**	**P.Wessels [2]**			
64. **P.Wessels [2]** (NED)	6/2 6/2	6/1 4/6 7/5			

V.Voltchkov [6] 6/4 1/6 6/3

V.Voltchkov [6] 3/6 6/2 6/3

THE BOYS' DOUBLES CHAMPIONSHIP

Holders: M. Lee and J. M. Trotman

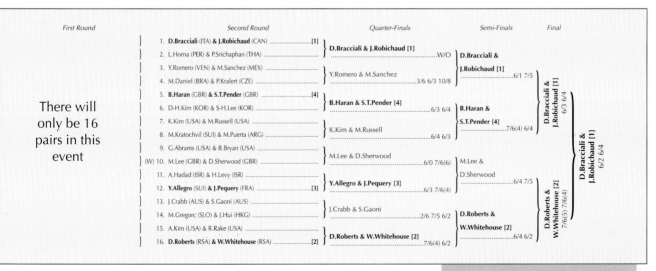

First Round	Second Round	Quarter-Finals	Semi-Finals	Final
	1. **D.Bracciali (ITA) & J.Robichaud (CAN) [1]**	**D.Bracciali & J.Robichaud [1]**		
	2. L.Horna (PER) & P.Srichaphan (THA)	W/O	**D.Bracciali &**	
	3. Y.Romero (VEN) & M.Sanchez (MEX)	Y.Romero & M.Sanchez	**J.Robichaud [1]**	
	4. M.Daniel (BRA) & P.Kralert (CZE)	3/6 6/3 10/8	6/1 7/5	
	5. **B.Haran (GBR) & S.T.Pender (GBR) [4]**	**B.Haran & S.T.Pender [4]**		
	6. D-H.Kim (KOR) & S-H.Lee (KOR)	6/3 6/4	**B.Haran &**	
There will only be 16 pairs in this event	7. K.Kim (USA) & M.Russell (USA)	K.Kim & M.Russell	**S.T.Pender [4]**	**D.Bracciali &**
	8. M.Kratochvil (SUI) & M.Puerta (ARG)	6/4 6/3	7/6(4) 6/4	**J.Robichaud [1]**
	9. G.Abrams (USA) & B.Bryan (USA)	M.Lee & D.Sherwood		6/3 6/4
	(W) 10. M.Lee (GBR) & D.Sherwood (GBR)	6/0 7/6(6)	M.Lee &	
	11. A.Hadad (ISR) & H.Levy (ISR)	**Y.Allegro & J.Pequery [3]**	D.Sherwood	
	12. **Y.Allegro (SUI) & J.Pequery (FRA) [3]**	6/3 7/6(4)	6/4 7/5	
	13. J.Crabb (AUS) & S.Gaoni (AUS)	J.Crabb & S.Gaoni		
	14. M.Gregorc (SLO) & J.Hui (HKG)	2/6 7/5 6/2	**D.Roberts &**	
	15. A.Kim (USA) & R.Rake (USA)	**D.Roberts & W.Whitehouse [2]**	**W.Whitehouse [2]**	
	16. **D.Roberts (RSA) & W.Whitehouse (RSA) [2]**	7/6(4) 6/2	6/4 6/2	

D.Bracciali & J.Robichaud [1] 6/2 6/4

D.Roberts & W.Whitehouse [2] 7/6(5) 7/6(4)

For both the Girls' Singles *and* the Girls' Doubles Championships, the winners become the holders, for the year only, of a Cup presented by the All England Lawn Tennis and Croquet Club. The winners each receive a miniature Cup and the runners-up receive mementoes.

Holder: Miss A. Olsza

First Round	Second Round	Third Round	Quarter-Finals	Semi-Finals	Final
1. **Miss M.Grzybowska [1]** ....(POL)	**Miss M.Grzybowska [1]**				
2. Miss A.Rippner......................(USA)	......................6/4 6/2	**Miss M.Grzybowska [1]**			
3. Miss S.Nacuk.......................(YUG)	Miss J.Wohr	......................6/3 3/6 6/2			
4. Miss J.Wohr.........................(GER)	......................6/2 6/2		**Miss M.Grzybowska [1]**		
5. Miss N.Hubnerova..................(CZE)	Miss E.Koulikovskaya		......................6/4 4/6 7/5		
6. Miss E.Koulikovskaya.............(RUS)	......................6/3 6/4	**Miss M.Lucic [12]**			
7. Miss L.Perkins......................(GBR)	**Miss M.Lucic [12]**	......................7/6 6/4			
8. **Miss M.Lucic [12]** ....(CRO)	......................6/0 6/2			**Miss A.Mauresmo [10]**	
9. **Miss A.Mauresmo [10]** ....(FRA)	**Miss A.Mauresmo [10]**			......................6/2 6/4	
10. Miss M.Inoue......................(JPN)	......................6/2 6/3	**Miss A.Mauresmo [10]**			
11. Miss Y-J.Cho.......................(KOR)	Miss Y-J.Cho	......................6/4 6/2			
12. Miss A.Sebova.....................(SVK)	......................7/5 6/2		**Miss A.Mauresmo [10]**		
13. Miss C.Castano....................(COL)	Miss J.Steck		......................6/3 6/3		
14. Miss J.Steck........................(RSA)	......................6/3 6/2	Miss J.Steck			
15. Miss D.Gaviria.....................(PER)	**Miss S.E.Drake-Brockman [8]**	......................6/3 6/4			
16. **Miss S.E.Drake-Brockman [8]** ..(AUS)	......................6/1 6/2				
17. **Miss S.Kleinova [4]** ....(CZE)	**Miss S.Kleinova [4]**				
18. Miss A.Soukup.....................(CAN)	......................6/1 6/4	Miss A.Janes			
19. Miss A.Janes.......................(GBR)	Miss A.Janes	......................6/2 6/1			
20. Miss K.Tokuda.....................(USA)	......................6/4 6/3		**Miss O.Barabanschikova [11]**		
21. Miss K.Jagieniak...................(FRA)	Miss K.Jagieniak		......................6/2 6/0		
22. Miss C.Curran......................(IRL)	......................6/1 6/1	**Miss O.Barabanschikova [11]**			
23. Miss S.Urickova....................(SVK)	**Miss O.Barabanschikova [11]**	......................6/4 6/2			
24. **Miss O.Barabanschikova [11]** ..(BLR)	......................6/1 6/3			**Miss A-G.Sidot [5]**	
25. **Miss Z.Gubacsi [16]** ....(HUN)	**Miss Z.Gubacsi [16]**			......................6/7(1) 7/5 6/1	
26. Miss G.Casoni......................(ITA)	......................0/6 6/3 6/2	Miss L.Latimer			
27. Miss L.Latimer.....................(GBR)	Miss L.Latimer	......................6/4 6/4			
28. Miss A.Schwarz....................(SUI)	......................6/1 7/6(2)		**Miss A-G.Sidot [5]**		
29. Miss C.Black........................(ZIM)	Miss C.Black		......................6/3 6/0		
30. Miss M.White......................(USA)	......................3/6 6/0 6/0	**Miss A-G.Sidot [5]**			
31. Miss L.Bernal......................(PAR)	**Miss A-G.Sidot [5]**	......................6/2 5/7 6/1			
32. **Miss A-G.Sidot [5]** ....(FRA)	......................6/1 6/0				
33. **Miss A.Ellwood [6]** ....(AUS)	**Miss A.Ellwood [6]**				
34. Miss G.Volekova...................(SVK)	......................5/7 6/4 6/3	**Miss A.Ellwood [6]**			
35. Miss J.Choudhury..................(GBR)	Miss A.Morigami	......................6/4 6/3			
36. Miss A.Morigami...................(JPN)	......................7/5 6/4		Miss S.Reeves		
37. Miss S.de Beer.....................(RSA)	Miss S.de Beer		......................7/6(3) 1/6 6/2		
38. Miss A.Radeljevic..................(CRO)	......................6/4 6/2	Miss S.Reeves			
39. Miss S.Reeves......................(USA)	Miss S.Reeves	......................6/4 6/3			
40. **Miss F.Zuluaga [15]** ....(COL)	......................6/4 3/6 7/5			**Miss N.Dechy [3]**	
41. **Miss J.Schonfeldova [14]** ......(CZE)	**Miss J.Schonfeldova [14]**			......................6/3 7/5	
42. Miss P.Palencia....................(MEX)	......................7/5 6/4	Miss E.Roubanova			
43. Miss S.Kovacic.....................(GER)	Miss E.Roubanova	......................6/2 0/6 8/6			
44. Miss E.Roubanova.................(GBR)	......................1/6 6/3 6/0		**Miss N.Dechy [3]**		
45. Miss C.Popescu....................(CAN)	Miss K.Marosi		......................6/3 6/1		
46. Miss K.Marosi......................(HUN)	......................6/0 7/6(2)	**Miss N.Dechy [3]**			
47. Miss K.Triska.......................(SWE)	**Miss N.Dechy [3]**	......................6/0 6/2			
48. **Miss N.Dechy [3]** ....(FRA)	......................4/6 6/3 6/3				
49. **Miss A.Cocheteux [7]** ....(FRA)	**Miss A.Cocheteux [7]**				
50. Miss R.Teperberg..................(ISR)	......................6/3 6/2	**Miss A.Cocheteux [7]**			
51. Miss T.Poutchek...................(BLR)	Miss T.Poutchek	......................6/2 6/4			
52. Miss K.Srebotnik..................(SLO)	......................6/4 7/5		Miss M.Serna		
53. Miss M.Kovacevic.................(CRO)	Miss K.Straczy		......................6/2 7/6(3)		
54. Miss K.Straczy.....................(POL)	......................6/4 6/4	Miss M.Serna			
55. Miss M.Serna.......................(ESP)	Miss M.Serna	......................6/2 6/2			
56. **Miss L.Osterloh [13]** ....(USA)	......................6/4 6/2			Miss M.Serna	
57. **Miss M.Jeon [9]** ....(KOR)	**Miss M.Jeon [9]**			......................6/4 6/7(4) 6/2	
58. Miss Z.Ondraskova................(CZE)	......................6/2 6/1	**Miss M.Jeon [9]**			
59. Miss I.Seljutina....................(KAZ)	Miss A.Tordoff	......................6/2 6/3			
60. Miss A.Tordoff.....................(GBR)	......................6/2 6/1		**Miss M.Jeon [9]**		
61. Miss Z.Valekova....................(SVK)	Miss Z.Valekova		......................6/1 3/6 6/2		
62. Miss J.Lehnhoff....................(USA)	......................6/1 6/2	Miss Z.Valekova			
63. Miss R.Sandu.......................(ROM)	**Miss P.Schnyder [2]**	......................6/4 7/5			
64. **Miss P.Schnyder [2]** ....(SUI)	......................6/2 6/0				

Winner (from right column):
Miss M.Grzybowska [1]

Miss A.Mauresmo [10] 6/2 6/4

Miss A.Mauresmo [10] 6/4 6/3

Miss A.Mauresmo [10] 4/6 6/3 6/4

Miss M.Serna 7/6(3) 6/1

Miss N.Dechy [3] 6/3 7/5

Holders: Miss C. Black and Miss A. Olsza

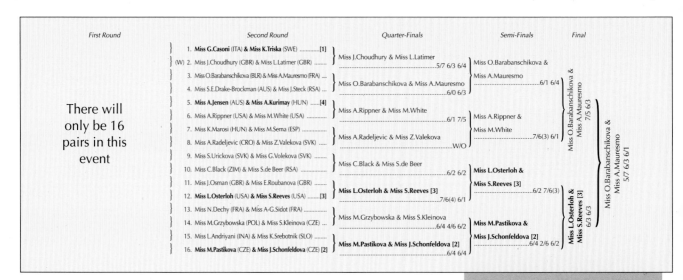

There will only be 16 pairs in this event

First Round	Second Round	Quarter-Finals	Semi-Finals	Final
	1. **Miss G.Casoni** (ITA) & **Miss K.Triska** (SWE) ......[1]	Miss J.Choudhury & Miss L.Latimer		
	(W) 2. Miss J.Choudhury (GBR) & Miss L.Latimer (GBR)	......................5/7 6/3 6/4	Miss O.Barabanschikova & Miss A.Mauresmo	
	3. Miss O.Barabanschikova (BLR) & Miss A.Mauresmo (FRA)	Miss O.Barabanschikova & Miss A.Mauresmo	......................6/1 6/4	
	4. Miss S.E.Drake-Brockman (AUS) & Miss J.Steck (RSA) ...	......................6/0 6/3		
	5. **Miss A.Jensen** (AUS) & **Miss A.Kurimay** (HUN) ......[4]	Miss A.Rippner & Miss M.White		Miss O.Barabanschikova & Miss A.Mauresmo 7/5 6/3
	6. Miss A.Rippner (USA) & Miss M.White (USA)	......................6/1 7/5	Miss A.Rippner & Miss M.White	
	7. Miss K.Marosi (HUN) & Miss M.Serna (ESP)	Miss A.Radeljevic & Miss Z.Valekova	......................7/6(3) 6/1	
	8. Miss A.Radeljevic (CRO) & Miss Z.Valekova (SVK)	......................W/O		
	9. Miss S.Urickova (SVK) & Miss G.Volekova (SVK)	Miss C.Black & Miss S.de Beer		Miss O.Barabanschikova & Miss A.Mauresmo 5/7 6/3 6/1
	10. Miss C.Black (ZIM) & Miss S.de Beer (RSA)	......................6/2 6/2	**Miss L.Osterloh & Miss S.Reeves [3]**	
	11. Miss J.Osman (GBR) & Miss E.Roubanova (GBR)	**Miss L.Osterloh & Miss S.Reeves [3]**	......................6/2 7/6(3)	
	12. **Miss L.Osterloh** (USA) & **Miss S.Reeves** (USA) ......[3]	......................7/6(4) 6/1		
	13. Miss N.Dechy (FRA) & Miss A-G.Sidot (FRA)	Miss M.Grzybowska & Miss S.Kleinova		**Miss L.Osterloh & Miss S.Reeves [3]** 6/3 6/3
	14. Miss M.Grzybowska (POL) & Miss S.Kleinova (CZE)	......................6/4 4/6 6/2	**Miss M.Pastikova & Miss J.Schonfeldova [2]**	
	15. Miss L.Andriyani (INA) & Miss K.Srebotnik (SLO)	**Miss M.Pastikova & Miss J.Schonfeldova [2]**	......................6/4 2/6 6/2	
	16. **Miss M.Pastikova** (CZE) & **Miss J.Schonfeldova** (CZE) [2]	......................6/4 6/4		

Champions and Runners-up

1877 - S. W. Gore
W. C. Marshall

1878 - P. F. Hadow
S. W. Gore

* 1879 - J. T. Hartley
V. St. L. Goold

1880 - J. T. Hartley
H. F. Lawford

1881 - W. Renshaw
J. T. Hartley

1882 - W. Renshaw
E. Renshaw

1883 - W. Renshaw
E. Renshaw

1884 - W. Renshaw
H. F. Lawford

1885 - W. Renshaw
H. F. Lawford

1886 - W. Renshaw
H. F. Lawford

* 1887 - H. F. Lawford
E. Renshaw

1888 - E. Renshaw
H. F. Lawford

1889 - W. Renshaw
E. Renshaw

1890 - W. J. Hamilton
W. Renshaw

* 1891 - W. Baddeley
J. Pim

1892 - W. Baddeley
J. Pim

1893 - J. Pim
W. Baddeley

1894 - J. Pim
W. Baddeley

* 1895 - W. Baddeley
W. V. Eaves

1896 - H. S. Mahony
W. Baddeley

1897 - R. F. Doherty
H. S. Mahony

1898 - R. F. Doherty
H. L . Doherty

1899 - R. F. Doherty
A. W. Gore

1900 - R. F. Doherty
S. H. Smith

1901 - A. W. Gore
R. F. Doherty

1902 - H. L. Doherty
A. W. Gore

1903 - H. L. Doherty
F. L. Riseley

1904 - H. L. Doherty
F. L. Riseley

1905 - H. L. Doherty
N. E. Brookes

1906 - H. L. Doherty
F. L. Riseley

* 1907 - N. E. Brookes
A. W. Gore

* 1908 - A. W. Gore
H. Roper Barrett

1909 - A. W. Gore
M. J. G. Ritchie

1910 - A. F. Wilding
A. W. Gore

1911 - A. F. Wilding
H. Roper Barrett

1912 - A. F. Wilding
A. W. Gore

1913 - A. F. Wilding
M. E. McLoughlin

1914 - N. E. Brookes
A. F. Wilding

1919 - G. L. Patterson
N. E. Brookes

1920 - W. T. Tilden
G. L. Patterson

1921 - W. T. Tilden
B. I. C. Norton

*† 1922 - G. L. Patterson
R. Lycett

1923 - W. M. Johnston
F. T. Hunter

1924 - J. Borotra
R. Lacoste

1925 - R. Lacoste
J. Borotra

1926 - J. Borotra
H. Kinsey

1927 - H. Cochet
J. Borotra

1928 - R. Lacoste
H. Cochet

1929 - H. Cochet
J. Borotra

1930 - W. T. Tilden
W. Allison

1931 - S. B. Wood
F. X. Shields

1932 - H. E. Vines
H. W. Austin

1933 - J. H. Crawford
H. E. Vines

1934 - F. J. Perry
J. H. Crawford

1935 - F. J. Perry
G. von Cramm

1936 - F. J. Perry
G. von Cramm

* 1937 - J. D. Budge
G. von Cramm

1938 - J. D. Budge
H. W. Austin

* 1939 - R. L. Riggs
E. T. Cooke

* 1946 - Y. Petra
G. E. Brown

1947 - J. Kramer
T. Brown

* 1948 - R. Falkenburg
J. E. Bromwich

1949 - F. R. Schroeder
J. Drobny

* 1950 - B. Patty
F. A. Sedgman

1951 - R. Savitt
K. McGregor

1952 - F. A. Sedgman
J. Drobny

* 1953 - V. Seixas
K. Nielsen

1954 - J. Drobny
K. R. Rosewall

1955 - T. Trabert
K. Nielsen

* 1956 - L. A. Hoad
K. R. Rosewall

1957 - L. A. Hoad
A. J. Cooper

* 1958 - A. J. Cooper
N. A. Fraser

* 1959 - A. Olmedo
R. Laver

* 1960 - N. A. Fraser
R. Laver

1961 - R. Laver
C. R. McKinley

1962 - R. Laver
M. F. Mulligan

* 1963 - C. R. McKinley
F. S. Stolle

1964 - R. Emerson
F. S. Stolle

1965 - R. Emerson
F. S. Stolle

1966 - M. Santana
R. D. Ralston

1967 - J. D. Newcombe
W. P. Bungert

1968 - R. Laver
A. D. Roche

1969 - R. Laver
J. D. Newcombe

1970 - J. D. Newcombe
K. R. Rosewall

1971 - J. D. Newcombe
S. R. Smith

* 1972 - S. R. Smith
I. Nastase

* 1973 - J. Kodes
A. Metreveli

1974 - J. S. Connors
K. R. Rosewall

1975 - A. R. Ashe
J. S. Connors

1976 - B. Borg
I. Nastase

1977 - B. Borg
J. S. Connors

1978 - B. Borg
J. S.Connors

1979 - B. Borg
R. Tanner

1980 - B. Borg
J. P. McEnroe

1981 - J. P. McEnroe
B. Borg

1982 - J. S. Connors
J. P. McEnroe

1983 - J. P. McEnroe
C. J. Lewis

1984 - J. P. McEnroe
J. S. Connors

1985 - B. Becker
K. Curren

1986 - B.Becker
I. Lendl

1987 - P. Cash
I. Lendl

1988 - S. Edberg
B. Becker

1989 - B. Becker
S. Edberg

1990 - S. Edberg
B. Becker

1991 - M. Stich
B. Becker

1992 - A. Agassi
G. Ivanisevic

1993 - P. Sampras
J. Courier

1994 - P. Sampras
G. Ivanisevic

1995 - P. Sampras
B. Becker

NOTE: For the years 1913, 1914 and 1919-23 inclusive the Championship Roll includes the 'World's Championship on Grass' granted to The Lawn Tennis Association by The International Lawn Tennis Federation. This title was then abolished and commencing in 1924 they became The Official Lawn Tennis Championships recognised by The International Lawn Tennis Federation. Prior to 1922 the holders in the singles events and the gentlemen's doubles did not compete in The Championships but met the winners of these events in the Challenge Rounds.
† Challenge Round abolished; holders subsequently played through. *The holder did not defend the title.

Champions and Runners-up

1884 - Miss M. Watson Miss L. Watson	† 1922 - Mlle. S. Lenglen Mrs. F. Mallory	* 1939 - Miss A. Marble Miss K. E. Stammers
1885 - Miss M. Watson Miss B. Bingley	1923 - Mlle. S. Lenglen Miss K. McKane	* 1946 - Miss P. Betz Miss L. Brough
1886 - Miss B. Bingley Miss M. Watson	1924 - Miss K. McKane Miss H. Wills	* 1947 - Miss M. Osborne Miss D. Hart
1887 - Miss L. Dod Miss B. Bingley	1925 - Mlle. S. Lenglen Miss J. Fry	1948 - Miss L. Brough Miss D. Hart
1888 - Miss L. Dod Mrs. G. W. Hillyard	1926 - Mrs. L. A. Godfree Sta. L. de Alvarez	1949 - Miss L. Brough Mrs. W. du Pont
* 1889 - Mrs. G. W. Hillyard Miss L. Rice	* 1927 - Miss H. Wills Sta. L. de Alvarez	1950 - Miss L. Brough Mrs. W. du Pont
* 1890 - Miss L. Rice Miss M. Jacks	1928 - Miss H. Wills Sta. L. de Alvarez	1951 - Miss D. Hart Miss S. Fry

| 1891 - Miss L. Dod
Mrs. G. W. Hillyard |
| 1892 - Miss L. Dod
Mrs. G. W. Hillyard |
| 1893 - Miss L. Dod
Mrs. G. W. Hillyard |
| * 1894 - Mrs. G. W. Hillyard
Miss E. L. Austin |
| * 1895 - Miss C. Cooper
Miss H. Jackson |
| 1896 - Miss C. Cooper
Mrs. W. H.Pickering |
| 1897 - Mrs. G. W. Hillyard
Miss C. Cooper |
| * 1898 - Miss C. Cooper
Miss L Martin |
| 1899 - Mrs. G. W. Hillyard
Miss C. Cooper |
| 1900 - Mrs. G. W. Hillyard
Miss C. Cooper |
| 1901 - Mrs. A. Sterry
Mrs. G. W. Hillyard |
| 1902 - Miss M. E. Robb
Mrs. A. Sterry |
| * 1903 - Miss D. K. Douglass
Miss E. W. Thomson |
| 1904 - Miss D. K. Douglass
Mrs. A. Sterry |
| 1905 - Miss M. Sutton
Miss D. K. Douglass |
| 1906 - Miss D. K Douglass
Miss M. Sutton |
| 1907 - Miss M. Sutton
Mrs. Lambert Chambers |
| * 1908 - Mrs. A. Sterry
Miss A. M. Morton |
| * 1909 - Miss D. P. Boothby
Miss A. M. Morton |
| 1910 - Mrs. Lambert Chambers
Miss D. P. Boothby |
| 1911 - Mrs. Lambert Chambers
Miss D. P. Boothby |
| * 1912 - Mrs. D. R. Larcombe
Mrs. A. Sterry |
| * 1913 - Mrs. Lambert Chambers
Mrs. R. J. McNair |
| 1914 - Mrs. Lambert Chambers
Mrs. D. R. Larcombe |
| 1919 - Mlle. S. Lenglen
Mrs. Lambert Chambers |
| 1920 - Mlle. S. Lenglen
Mrs. Lambert Chambers |
| 1921 - Mlle. S. Lenglen
Miss E. Ryan |

1929 - Miss H. Wills Miss H. H. Jacobs	1952 - Miss M. Connolly Miss L. Brough
1930 - Mrs. F. S. Moody Miss E. Ryan	1953 - Miss M. Connolly Miss D. Hart
* 1931 - Fraulein C. Aussem Fraulein H. Krahwinkel	1954 - Miss M. Connolly Miss L. Brough
1932 - Mrs. F. S. Moody Miss H. H. Jacobs	* 1955 - Miss L. Brough Mrs. J. G. Fleitz
1933 - Mrs. F. S. Moody Miss D. E. Round	1956 - Miss S. Fry Miss A. Buxton
* 1934 - Miss D. E. Round Miss H. H. Jacobs	* 1957 - Miss A. Gibson Miss D. R. Hard
1935 - Mrs. F. S. Moody Miss H. H. Jacobs	1958 - Miss A. Gibson Miss A. Mortimer
* 1936 - Miss H. H. Jacobs Frau. S. Sperling	* 1959 - Miss M. E. Bueno Miss D. R. Hard
1937 - Miss D. E. Round Miss J. Jedrzejowska	1960 - Miss M. E. Bueno Miss S. Reynolds
* 1938 - Mrs. F. S. Moody Miss H. H. Jacobs	* 1961 - Miss A. Mortimer Miss C. C. Truman

1962 - Mrs. J. R. Susman Mrs. V. Sukova
* 1963 - Miss M. Smith Miss B. J. Moffitt
1964 - Miss M. E. Bueno Miss M. Smith
1965 - Miss M. Smith Miss M. E. Bueno
1966 - Mrs. L. W. King Miss M. E. Bueno
1967 - Mrs. L. W. King Mrs. P. F. Jones
1968 - Mrs. L. W. King Miss J. A. M. Tegart
1969 - Mrs. P. F. Jones Mrs. L. W. King
* 1970 - Mrs. B. M. Court Mrs. L. W. King
1971 - Miss E. F. Goolagong Mrs. B. M. Court
1972 - Mrs. L. W. King Miss E. F. Goolagong
1973 - Mrs. L. W. King Miss C. M. Evert
1974 - Miss C. M. Evert Mrs. O. Morozova
1975 - Mrs. L. W. King Mrs. R. Cawley
* 1976 - Miss C. M. Evert Mrs. R. Cawley
1977 - Miss S. V. Wade Miss B. F. Stove
1978 - Miss M. Navratilova Miss C. M. Evert
1979 - Miss M. Navratilova Mrs. J. M. Lloyd
1980 - Mrs. R. Cawley Mrs. J. M. Lloyd
1981 - Mrs. J. M. Lloyd Miss H. Mandlikova
1982 - Miss M. Navratilova Mrs. J. M. Lloyd
1983 - Miss M. Navratilova Miss A. Jaeger
1984 - Miss M. Navratilova Mrs. J. M. Lloyd
1985 - Miss M. Navratilova Mrs. J. M. Lloyd
1986 - Miss M. Navratilova Miss H. Mandlikova
1987 - Miss M. Navratilova Miss S. Graf
1988 - Miss S. Graf Miss M. Navratilova
1989 - Miss S. Graf Miss M. Navratilova
1990 - Miss M. Navratilova Miss Z. Garrison
1991 - Miss S. Graf Miss G. Sabatini
1992 - Miss S. Graf Miss M. Seles
1993 - Miss S. Graf Miss J. Novotna
1994 - Miss C. Martinez Miss M. Navratilova
1995 - Miss S. Graf Miss A. Sanchez Vicario

MAIDEN NAMES OF LADY CHAMPIONS

In the tables the following have been recorded
in both married and single identities.

Mrs. R. Cawley	Miss E. F. Goolagong		Mrs. F. S. Moody	Miss H. Wills
Mrs. Lambert Chambers	Miss D. K. Douglass		Mrs. O. Morozova	Miss O. Morozova
Mrs. B. M. Court	Miss M. Smith	Mrs. G. W. Hillyard	Miss B. Bingley	Mrs. L. E. G. Price	Miss S. Reynolds
Mrs. B. C. Covell	Miss P. L. Howkins	Mrs. P. F. Jones	Miss A. S. Haydon	Mrs. G. E. Reid	Miss K. Melville
Mrs. D. E. Dalton	Miss J. A. M. Tegart	Mrs. L. W. King	Miss B. J. Moffitt	Mrs. P. D. Smylie	Miss E. M. Sayers
Mrs. W. du Pont	Miss M. Osborne	Mrs. M. R. King	Miss P. E. Mudford	Frau. S. Sperling	Fraulein H. Krahwinkel
Mrs. L. A. Godfree	Miss K. McKane	Mrs. D. R. Larcombe	Miss E. W. Thomson	Mrs. A. Sterry	Miss C. Cooper
Mrs. H. F. Gourlay Cawley	Miss H. F. Gourlay	Mrs. J. M. Lloyd	Miss C. M. Evert	Mrs. J. R. Susman	Miss K. Hantze

MEN'S DOUBLES

1879 - L. R. Erskine and H. F. Lawford
F. Durant and G. E. Tabor
1880 - W. Renshaw and E. Renshaw
O. E. Woodhouse and C. J. Cole
1881 - W. Renshaw and E. Renshaw
W. J. Down and H. Vaughan
1882 - J. T. Hartley and R. T. Richardson
J. G. Horn and C. B. Russell
1883 - C. W. Grinstead and C. E. Welldon
C. B. Russell and R. T. Milford
1884 - W. Renshaw and E. Renshaw
E. W. Lewis and E.L Williams
1885 - W. Renshaw and E. Renshaw
C. E. Farrer and A. J. Stanley
1886 - W. Renshaw and E. Renshaw
C. E. Farrer and A. J. Stanley
1887 - P. Bowes-Lyon and H. W. W. Wilberforce
J. H. Crispe and E. Barratt Smith
1888 - W. Renshaw and E. Renshaw
P Bowes-Lyon and H. W. W. Wilberforce
1889 - W. Renshaw and E. Renshaw
E. W. Lewis and G. W. Hillyard
1890 - J. Pim and F. O. Stoker
E. W. Lewis and G. W. Hillyard
1891 - W. Baddeley and H. Baddeley
J. Pim and F. O. Stoker
1892 - H. S. Barlow and E. W. Lewis
W. Baddeley and H. Baddeley
1893 - J. Pim and F. O. Stoker
E. W. Lewis and H. S. Barlow
1894 - W. Baddeley and H. Baddeley
H. S. Barlow and C. H. Martin
1895 - W. Baddeley and H. Baddeley
E. W. Lewis and W. V. Eaves
1896 - W. Baddeley and H. Baddeley
R. F. Doherty and H. A. Nisbet
1897 - R. F. Doherty and H. L. Doherty
W. Baddeley and H. Baddeley
1898 - R. F. Doherty and H. L . Doherty
H. A. Nisbet and C. Hobart
1899 - R. F. Doherty and H. L. Doherty
H. A. Nisbet and C. Hobart
1900 - R. F. Doherty and H. L. Doherty
H. Roper Barrett and H. A. Nisbet
1901 - R. F. Doherty and H. L. Doherty
Dwight Davis and Holcombe Ward
1902 - S. H. Smith and F. L. Riseley
R. F. Doherty and H. L. Doherty
1903 - R. F. Doherty and H. L. Doherty
S. H. Smith and F. L. Riseley
1904 - R. F. Doherty and H. L. Doherty
S. H. Smith and F. L. Riseley
1905 - R. F. Doherty and H. L. Doherty
S. H. Smith and F. L. Riseley
1906 - S. H. Smith and F. L. Riseley
R. F. Doherty and H. L. Doherty
1907 - N. E. Brookes and A. F. Wilding
B. C. Wright and K. H. Behr
1908 - A. F. Wilding and M. J. G. Ritchie
A. W. Gore and H. Roper Barrett
1909 - A. W. Gore and H. Roper Barrett
S. N. Doust and H. A. Parker
1910 - A. F. Wilding and M. J. G. Ritchie
A. W. Gore and H. Roper Barrett
1911 - M. Decugis and A. H. Gobert
M. J. G. Ritchie and A. F. Wilding
1912 - H. Roper Barrett and C. P. Dixon
M. Decugis and A. H. Gobert
1913 - H. Roper Barrett and C. P. Dixon
F. W. Rahe and H. Kleinschroth
1914 - N. E. Brookes and A. F. Wilding
H. Roper Barrett and C. P. Dixon
1919 - R. V. Thomas and P. O'Hara-Wood
R. Lycett and R. W. Heath
1920 - R. N. Williams and C. S. Garland
A. R. F. Kingscote and J. C. Parke
1921 - R. Lycett and M. Woosnam
F. G. Lowe and A. H. Lowe
1922 - R. Lycett and J. O. Anderson
G. L. Patterson and P. O'Hara-Wood
1923 - R. Lycett and L. A. Godfree
Count de Gomar and E. Flaquer
1924 - F. T. Hunter and V. Richards
R. N. Williams and W. M. Washburn
1925 - J. Borotra and R. Lacoste
J. Hennessey and R. Casey
1926 - H. Cochet and J. Brugnon
V. Richards and H. Kinsey
1927 - F. T. Hunter and W. T. Tilden
J. Brugnon and H. Cochet
1928 - H. Cochet and J. Brugnon
G. L. Patterson and J. B. Hawkes
1929 - W. Allison and J. Van Ryn
J. C. Gregory and I. G. Collins
1930 - W. Allison and J. Van Ryn
J. H. Doeg and G. M. Lott
1931 - G. M Lott and J. Van Ryn
H. Cochet and J. Brugnon
1932 - J. Borotra and J. Brugnon
G. P. Hughes and F. J. Perry
1933 - J. Borotra and J. Brugnon
R. Nunoi and J. Satoh
1934 - G. M. Lott and L. R. Stoefen
J. Borotra and J. Brugnon
1935 - J. H. Crawford and A. K . Quist
W. Allison and J. Van Ryn
1936 - G. P. Hughes and C. R. D. Tuckey
C. E. Hare and F. H. D. Wilde
1937 - J. D. Budge and G. Mako
G. P. Hughes and C. R. D. Tuckey
1938 - J. D. Budge and G. Mako
H. Henkel and G. von Metaxa
1939 - R. L. Riggs and E. T. Cooke
C. E. Hare and F. H. D. Wilde
1946 - T. Brown and J. Kramer
G. E. Brown and D. Pails
1947 - R. Falkenburg and J. Kramer
A. J. Mottram and O. W. Sidwell
1948 - J. E. Bromwich and F. A. Sedgman
T. Brown and G. Mulloy
1949 - R. Gonzales and F. Parker
G. Mulloy and F. R. Schroeder
1950 - J. E. Bromwich and A. K. Quist
G. E. Brown and O. W Sidwell
1951 - K. McGregor and F. A. Sedgman
J. Drobny and E. W. Sturgess
1952 - K. McGregor and F. A. Sedgman
V. Seixas and E. W. Sturgess
1953 - L. A. Hoad and K. R. Rosewall
R. N. Hartwig and M. G. Rose
1954 - R. N. Hartwig and M. G. Rose
V. Seixas and T. Trabert
1955 - R. N. Hartwig and L. A. Hoad
N. A. Fraser and K. R. Rosewall
1956 - L. A. Hoad and K. R. Rosewall
N. Pietrangeli and O. Sirola
1957 - G. Mulloy and B. Patty
N. A. Fraser and L. A. Hoad
1958 - S. Davidson and U. Schmidt
A. J. Cooper and N. A. Fraser
1959 - R. Emerson and N. A. Fraser
R. Laver and R. Mark
1960 - R. H. Osuna and R. D. Ralston
M. G. Davies and R. K. Wilson
1961 - R. Emerson and N. A. Fraser
R. A. J. Hewitt and F. S. Stolle
1962 - R. A. J. Hewitt and F. S. Stolle
B. Jovanovic and N. Pilic
1963 - R. H. Osuna and A. Palafox
J. C. Barclay and P. Darmon
1964 - R. A. J. Hewitt and F. S. Stolle
R. Emerson and K. N. Fletcher
1965 - J. D. Newcombe and A. D. Roche
K. N. Fletcher and R. A. J. Hewitt
1966 - K. N. Fletcher and J. D. Newcombe
W. W. Bowrey and O. K. Davidson
1967 - R. A. J. Hewitt and F. D. McMillan
R. Emerson and K. N. Fletcher
1968 - J. D. Newcombe and A. D. Roche
K. R. Rosewall and F. S. Stolle
1969 - J. D. Newcombe and A. D. Roche
T. S. Okker and M. C. Reissen
1970 - J. D. Newcombe and A. D. Roche
K. R. Rosewall and F. S. Stolle
1971 - R. S. Emerson and R. G. Laver
A. R. Ashe and R. D. Ralston
1972 - R. A. J. Hewitt and F. D. McMillan
S. R. Smith and E. J. van Dillen
1973 - J. S. Connors and I. Nastase
J. R. Cooper and N. A. Fraser
1974 - J. D. Newcombe and A. D. Roche
R. C. Lutz and S. R. Smith
1975 - V. Gerulaitis and A. Mayer
C. Dowdeswell and A. J. Stone
1976 - B. E. Gottfried and R. Ramirez
R. L. Case and G. Masters
1977 - R. L. Case and G. Masters
J. G. Alexander and P. C. Dent
1978 - R. A. J. Hewitt and F. D. McMillan
P. Fleming and J. P. McEnroe
1979 - P. Fleming and J. P . McEnroe
B. E. Gottfried and R. Ramirez
1980 - P. McNamara and P. McNamee
R. C. Lutz and S. R. Smith
1981 - P. Fleming and J. P. McEnroe
R. C. Lutz and S. R. Smith
1982 - P. McNamara and P. McNamee
P. Fleming and J. P. McEnroe
1983 - P. Fleming and J. P McEnroe
T. E. Gullikson and T. R. Gullikson
1984 - P. Fleming and J. P. McEnroe
P. Cash and P. McNamee
1985 - H. P. Guenthardt and B. Taroczy
P. Cash and J. B. Fitzgerald
1986 - J. Nystrom and M. Wilander
G. Donnelly and P. Fleming
1987 - K. Flach and R. Seguso
S. Casal and E. Sanchez
1988 - K. Flach and R. Seguso
J. B. Fitzgerald and A. Jarryd
1989 - J. B. Fitzgerald and A. Jarryd
R. Leach and J. Pugh
1990 - R. Leach and J. Pugh
P. Aldrich and D. T. Visser
1991 - J. B. Fitzgerald and A. Jarryd
J. Frana and L. Lavalle
1992 - J. P. McEnroe and M. Stich
J. Grabb and R. A. Reneberg
1993 - T. A. Woodbridge and M. Woodforde
G. Connell and P. Galbraith
1994 - T. A. Woodbridge and M. Woodforde
G. Connell and P. Galbraith
1995 - T. A. Woodbridge and M. Woodforde
R. Leach and S. Melville

LADIES' DOUBLES

1913 - Mrs. R. J. McNair and Miss D. P. Boothby
Mrs. A. Sterry and Mrs. Lambert Chambers
1914 - Miss E. Ryan and Miss A. M. Morton
Mrs. D. R. Larcombe and Mrs. F. J. Hannam
1919 - Mlle. S. Lenglen and Miss E. Ryan
Mrs. Lambert Chambers and Mrs. D. R. Larcombe
1920 - Mlle. S. Lenglen and Miss E. Ryan
Mrs. Lambert Chambers and Mrs. D. R. Larcombe
1921 - Mlle. S. Lenglen and Miss E. Ryan
Mrs. A. E. Beamish and Mrs. G. E. Peacock
1922 - Mlle. S. Lenglen and Miss E. Ryan
Mrs. A. D. Stocks and Miss K. McKane
1923 - Mlle. S. Lenglen and Miss E. Ryan
Miss J. Austin and Miss E. L. Colyer
1924 - Mrs. H. Wightman and Miss H. Wills
Mrs. B. C. Covell and Miss K. McKane
1925 - Mlle. S. Lenglen and Miss E. Ryan
Mrs. A. V. Bridge and Mrs. C. G. Mcllquham
1926 - Miss E. Ryan and Miss M. K. Browne
Mrs. L. A. Godfree and Miss E. L. Colyer
1927 - Miss H. Wills and Miss E. Ryan
Miss E. L. Heine and Mrs. G. E. Peacock
1928 - Mrs. Holcroft-Watson and Miss P. Saunders
Miss E. H. Harvey and Miss E. Bennett
1929 - Mrs. Holcroft-Watson and Mrs. L. R. C. Michell
Mrs. B. C. Covell and Mrs. D. C. Shepherd-Barron
1930 - Mrs. F. S. Moody and Miss E. Ryan
Miss E. Cross and Miss S. Palfrey
1931 - Mrs. D. C. Shepherd-Barron and Miss P. E. Mudford
Mlle. D. Metaxa and Mlle. J. Sigart
1932 - Mlle. D. Metaxa and Mlle. J. Sigart
Miss E. Ryan and Miss H. H. Jacobs
1933 - Mme. R. Mathieu and Miss E. Ryan
Miss F. James and Miss A. M. Yorke
1934 - Mme. R. Mathieu and Miss E. Ryan
Mrs. D. Andrus and Mme. S. Henrotin
1935 - Miss F. James and Miss K. E. Stammers
Mme. R. Mathieu and Frau. S. Sperling
1936 - Miss F. James and Miss K. E. Stammers
Mrs. S. P. Fabyan and Miss H. H. Jacobs
1937 - Mme. R. Mathieu and Miss A. M. Yorke
Mrs. M. R. King and Mrs. J. B. Pittman
1938 - Mrs. S. P. Fabyan and Miss A. Marble
Mme. R. Mathieu and Miss A. M. Yorke
1939 - Mrs S. P. Fabyan and Miss A. Marble
Miss H. H. Jacobs and Miss A. M. Yorke
1946 - Miss L. Brough and Miss M. Osborne
Miss P. Betz and Miss D. Hart
1947 - Miss D. Hart and Mrs. P. C. Todd
Miss L. Brough and Miss M. Osborne
1948 - Miss L. Brough and Mrs. W. du Pont
Miss D. Hart and Mrs. P. C. Todd
1949 - Miss L. Brough and Mrs. W. du Pont
Miss G. Moran and Mrs. P. C. Todd
1950 - Miss L. Brough and Mrs. W. du Pont
Miss S. Fry and Miss D. Hart
1951 - Miss S. Fry and Miss D. Hart
Miss L. Brough and Mrs. W. du Pont
1952 - Miss S. Fry and Miss D. Hart
Miss L. Brough and Miss M. Connolly
1953 - Miss S. Fry and Miss D. Hart
Miss M. Connolly and Miss J. Sampson
1954 - Miss L. Brough and Mrs. W. du Pont
Miss S. Fry and Miss D. Hart
1955 - Miss A. Mortimer and Miss J. A. Shilcock
Miss S. J. Bloomer and Miss P. E. Ward
1956 - Miss A. Buxton and Miss A. Gibson
Miss F. Muller and Miss D. G. Seeney
1957 - Miss A. Gibson and Miss D. R. Hard
Mrs. K. Hawton and Mrs. T. D. Long
1958 - Miss M. E. Bueno and Miss A. Gibson
Mrs. W. du Pont and Miss M. Varner
1959 - Miss J. Arth and Miss D. R. Hard
Mrs. J. G. Fleitz and Miss C. C. Truman
1960 - Miss M. E. Bueno and Miss D. R. Hard
Miss S. Reynolds and Miss R. Schuurman
1961 - Miss K. Hantze and Miss B. J. Moffitt
Miss J. Lehane and Miss M. Smith
1962 - Miss B. J. Moffitt and Mrs. J. R. Susman
Mrs. L. E. G. Price and Miss R. Schuurman
1963 - Miss M. E. Bueno and Miss D. R. Hard
Miss R. A. Ebbern and Miss M. Smith
1964 - Miss M. Smith and Miss L. R. Turner
Miss B. J. Moffitt and Mrs. J. R. Susman
1965 - Miss M. E. Bueno and Miss B. J. Moffitt
Miss F. Durr and Miss J. Lieffrig
1966 - Miss M. E. Bueno and Miss N. Richey
Miss M. Smith and Miss J. A. M. Tegart
1967 - Miss R. Casals and Mrs. L. W. King
Miss M. E. Bueno and Miss N. Richey
1968 - Miss R. Casals and Mrs. L. W. King
Miss F. Durr and Mrs. P. F. Jones
1969 - Mrs. B. M. Court and Miss J. A. M. Tegart
Miss P. S. A. Hogan and Miss M. Michel
1970 - Miss R. Casals and Mrs. L. W. King
Miss F. Durr and Miss S. V. Wade
1971 - Miss R. Casals and Mrs. L. W. King
Mrs. B. M. Court and Miss E. F. Goolagong
1972 - Mrs. L. W. King and Miss B. F. Stove
Mrs. D. E. Dalton and Miss F. Durr
1973 - Miss R. Casals and Mrs. L. W. King
Miss F. Durr and Miss B. F. Stove
1974 - Miss E. F. Goolagong and Miss M. Michel
Miss H. F. Gourlay and Miss K. M. Krantzcke
1975 - Miss A. Kiyomura and Miss K. Sawamatsu
Miss F. Durr and Miss B. F. Stove
1976 - Miss C. M. Evert and Miss M. Navratilova
Mrs. L. W. King and Miss B. F. Stove
1977 - Mrs. H. F. Gourlay Cawley and Miss J. C. Russell
Miss M. Navratilova and Miss B. F . Stove
1978 - Mrs. G. E. Reid and Miss. W. M. Turnbull
Miss M. Jausovec and Miss V. Ruzici
1979 - Mrs. L. W. King and Miss M. Navratilova
Miss B. F. Stove and Miss W. M. Turnbull
1980 - Miss K. Jordan and Miss A. E. Smith
Miss R. Casals and Miss W. M. Turnbull
1981 - Miss M. Navratilova and Miss P. H. Shriver
Miss K. Jordan and Miss A. E. Smith
1982 - Miss M. Navratilova and Miss P. H. Shriver
Miss K. Jordan and Miss A. E. Smith
1983 - Miss M. Navratilova and Miss P. H. Shriver
Miss R. Casals and Miss W. M. Turnbull
1984 - Miss M. Navratilova and Miss P. H. Shriver
Miss K. Jordan and Miss A. E. Smith
1985 - Miss K. Jordan and Mrs. P. D. Smylie
Miss M. Navratilova and Miss P. H. Shriver
1986 - Miss M. Navratilova and Miss P. H. Shriver
Miss H. Mandlikova and Miss W. M. Turnbull
1987 - Miss C. Kohde-Kilsch and Miss H. Sukova
Miss B. Nagelsen and Mrs. P. D. Smylie
1988 - Miss S. Graf and Miss G. Sabatini
Miss L. Savchenko and Miss N. Zvereva
1989 - Miss J. Novotna and Miss H. Sukova
Miss L. Savchenko and Miss N. Zvereva
1990 - Miss J. Novotna and Miss H. Sukova
Miss K. Jordan and Mrs. P. D. Smylie
1991 - Miss L. Savchenko and Miss N. Zvereva
Miss G. Fernandez and Miss J. Novotna
1992 - Miss G. Fernandez and Miss N. Zvereva
Miss J. Novotna and Mrs. L. Savchenko-Neiland
1993 - Miss G. Fernandez and Miss N. Zvereva
Mrs. L. Neiland and Miss J. Novotna
1994 - Miss G. Fernandez and Miss N. Zvereva
Miss J. Novotna and Miss A. Sanchez Vicario
1995 - Miss J. Novotna and Miss A. Sanchez Vicario
Miss G. Fernandez and Miss N. Zvereva

MIXED DOUBLES

1913 - Hope Crisp and Mrs. C. O. Tuckey
    J. C. Parke and Mrs. D. R. Larcombe
1914 - J. C. Parke and Mrs. D.R. Larcombe
    A. F. Wilding and Mlle. M. Broquedis
1919 - R. Lycett and Miss E. Ryan
    A. D. Prebble and Mrs. Lambert Chambers
1920 - G. L. Patterson and Mlle. S. Lenglen
    R. Lycett and Miss E. Ryan
1921 - R. Lycett and Miss E. Ryan
    M. Woosnam and Miss P. L. Howkins
1922 - P. O'Hara-Wood and Mlle. S. Lenglen
    R. Lycett and Miss E. Ryan
1923 - R. Lycett and Miss E. Ryan
    L. S. Deane and Mrs. D. C. Shepherd-Barron
1924 - J. B. Gilbert and Miss K. McKane
    L. A. Godfree and Mrs. D. C. Shepherd-Barron
1925 - J. Borotra and Mlle. S. Lenglen
    H. L. de Morpurgo and Miss E. Ryan
1926 - L. A. Godfree and Mrs. L. A. Godfree
    H. Kinsey and Miss M. K. Browne
1927 - F. T. Hunter and Miss E. Ryan
    L. A. Godfree and Mrs. L. A. Godfree
1928 - P. D. B. Spence and Miss E. Ryan
    J. Crawford and Miss D. Akhurst
1929 - F. T. Hunter and Miss H. Wills
    I. G. Collins and Miss J. Fry
1930 - J. H. Crawford and Miss E. Ryan
    D. Prenn and Fraulein H. Krahwinkel
1931 - G. M. Lott and Mrs L. A. Harper
    I. G. Collins and Miss J. C. Ridley
1932 - E. Maier and Miss E. Ryan
    H. C. Hopman and Mlle. J. Sigart
1933 - G. von Cramm and Fraulein H. Krahwinkel
    N. G. Farquharson and Miss M. Heeley
1934 - R. Miki and Miss D. E. Round
    H. W. Austin and Mrs D. C. Shepherd-Barron
1935 - F. J. Perry and Miss D. E. Round
    H. C. Hopman and Mrs. H. C. Hopman
1936 - F. J. Perry and Miss D. E. Round
    J. D. Budge and Mrs. S. P. Fabyan
1937 - J. D. Budge and Miss A. Marble
    Y. Petra and Mme. R. Mathieu
1938 - J. D. Budge and Miss A. Marble
    H. Henkel and Mrs. S. P. Fabyan
1939 - R. L. Riggs and Miss A. Marble
    F. H. D. Wilde and Miss N. B. Brown
1946 - T. Brown and Miss L. Brough
    G. E. Brown and Miss D. Bundy
1947 - J. E. Bromwich and Miss L. Brough

    C. F. Long and Mrs. N. M. Bolton
1948 - J. E. Bromwich and Miss L. Brough
    F. A. Sedgman and Miss D. Hart
1949 - E. W. Sturgess and Miss S. P. Summers
    J. E. Bromwich and Miss L. Brough
1950 - E. W. Sturgess and Miss L. Brough
    G. E. Brown and Mrs. P. C. Todd
1951 - F. A. Sedgman and Miss D. Hart
    M. G. Rose and Mrs. N. M. Bolton
1952 - F. A. Sedgman and Miss D. Hart
    E. Morea and Mrs. T. D. Long
1953 - V. Seixas and Miss D. Hart
    E. Morea and Miss S. Fry
1954 - V. Seixas and Miss D. Hart
    K. R. Rosewall and Mrs. W. du Pont
1955 - V. Seixas and Miss D. Hart
    E. Morea and Miss L. Brough
1956 - V. Seixas and Miss S. Fry
    G. Mulloy and Miss A. Gibson
1957 - M. G. Rose and Miss D. R. Hard
    N. A. Fraser and Miss A. Gibson
1958 - K. N. Howe and Miss L. Coghlan
    K. Nielsen and Miss A. Gibson
1959 - R. Laver and Miss D. R. Hard
    N. A. Fraser and Miss M. E. Bueno
1960 - R. Laver and Miss D. R. Hard
    R. N. Howe and Miss M. E. Bueno
1961 - F. S. Stolle and Miss L. R. Turner
    R. N. Howe and Miss E. Buding
1962 - N. A. Fraser and Mrs. W. du Pont
    R. D. Ralston and Miss A. S. Haydon
1963 - K. N. Fletcher and Miss M. Smith
    R. A. J. Hewitt and Miss D. R. Hard
1964 - F. S. Stolle and Miss L. R. Turner
    K. N. Fletcher and Miss M. Smith
1965 - K. N. Fletcher and Miss M. Smith
    A. D. Roche and Miss J. A. M. Tegart
1966 - K. N. Fletcher and Miss M. Smith
    R. D. Ralston and Mrs. L. W. King
1967 - O. K. Davidson and Mrs. L. W. King
    K. N. Fletcher and Miss M. E. Bueno
1968 - K. N. Fletcher and Mrs. B. M. Court
    A. Metreveli and Miss O. Morozova
1969 - F. S. Stolle and Mrs. P. F. Jones
    A. D. Roche and Miss J. A. M. Tegart
1970 - I. Nastase and Miss R. Casals
    A. Metreveli and Miss O. Morozova
1971 - O. K. Davidson and Mrs. L. W. King
    M. C. Riessen and Mrs. B. M. Court

1972 - I. Nastase and Miss R. Casals
    K.G. Warwick and Miss E. F. Goolagong
1973 - O. K. Davidson and Mrs. L. W. King
    R. Ramirez and Miss J. S. Newberry
1974 - O. K. Davidson and Mrs. L. W. King
    M. J. Farrell and Miss L. J. Charles
1975 - M. C. Riessen and Mrs. B. M. Court
    A. J. Stone and Miss B. F. Stove
1976 - A. D. Roche and Miss F. Durr
    R. L. Stockton and Miss R. Casals
1977 - R. A. J. Hewitt and Miss G. R. Stevens
    F. D. McMillan and Miss B. F. Stove
1978 - F. D. McMillan and Miss B. F. Stove
    R. O. Ruffels and Mrs. L. W. King
1979 - R. A. J. Hewitt and Miss G. R. Stevens
    F. D. McMillan and Miss B. F. Stove
1980 - J. R. Austin and Miss T. Austin
    M. R. Edmondson and Miss D. L. Fromholtz
1981 - F. D. McMillan and Miss B. F. Stove
    J. R. Austin and Miss T. Austin
1982 - K. Curren and Miss A. E. Smith
    J. M. Lloyd and Miss W. M. Turnbull
1983 - J. M. Lloyd and Miss W. M. Turnbull
    S. Denton and Mrs. L. W. King
1984 - J. M. Lloyd and Miss W. M. Turnbull
    S. Denton and Miss K. Jordan
1985 - P. McNamee and Miss M. Navratilova
    J. B. Fitzgerald and Mrs. P. D. Smylie
1986 - K. Flach and Miss K. Jordan
    H. P. Guenthardt and Miss M. Navratilova
1987 - M. J. Bates and Miss J. M. Durie
    D. Cahill and Miss N. Provis
1988 - S. E. Stewart and Miss Z. L. Garrison
    K. Jones and Mrs. S. W. Magers
1989 - J. Pugh and Miss J. Novotna
    M. Kratzmann and Miss J. M. Byrne
1990 - R. Leach and Miss Z. L. Garrison
    J. B. Fitzgerald and Mrs P. D. Smylie
1991 - J. B. Fitzgerald and Mrs. P. D. Smylie
    J. Pugh and Miss N. Zvereva
1992 - C. Suk and Mrs L. Savchenko-Neiland
    J. Eltingh and Miss M. Oremans
1993 - M. Woodforde and Miss M. Navratilova
    T. Nijssen and Miss M. M. Bollegraf
1994 - T. A. Woodbridge and Miss H. Sukova
    T. J. Middleton and Miss L. M. McNeil
1995 - J. Stark and Miss M. Navratilova
    C. Suk and Miss G. Fernandez

THE JUNIOR CHAMPIONSHIP ROLL

BOYS' SINGLES

1947 - K. Nielsen (Denmark)
1948 - S. Stockenberg (Sweden)
1949 - S. Stockenberg (Sweden)
1950 - J. A.T. Horn (G.B.)
1951 - J. Kupferburger (S.A.)
1952 - R. K. Wilson (G.B.)
1953 - W. A. Knight (G.B.)
1954 - R. Krishnan (India)
1955 - M. P. Hann (G.B.)
1956 - R. Holmberg (U.S.A.)
1957 - J. I. Tattersall (G.B.)
1958 - E. Buchholz (U.S.A.)
1959 - T. Lejus (U.S.S.R.)

1960 - A. R. Mandelstam (S.A.)
1961 - C. E. Graebner (U.S.A.)
1962 - S. Matthews (G.B.)
1963 - N. Kalogeropoulos (Greece)
1964 - I. El Shafei (U.A.R.)
1965 - V. Korotkov (U.S.S.R.)
1966 - V. Korotkov (U.S.S.R.)
1967 - M. Orantes (Spain)
1968 - J. G. Alexander (Australia)
1969 - B. Bertram (S.A.)
1970 - B. Bertram (S.A.)
1971 - R. Kreiss (U.S.A.)
1972 - B. Borg (Sweden)

1973 - W. Martin (U.S.A.)
1974 - W. Martin (U.S.A.)
1975 - C. J. Lewis (N.Z.)
1976 - H. Guenthardt (Switzerland)
1977 - V. A. Winitsky (U.S.A.)
1978 - I. Lendl (Czechoslovakia)
1979 - R. Krishnan (India)
1980 - T. Tulasne (France)
1981 - M. W. Anger (U.S.A.)
1982 - P. Cash (Australia)
1983 - S. Edberg (Sweden)
1984 - M.Kratzmann (Australia)
1985 - L. Lavalle (Mexico)

1986 - E. Velez (Mexico)
1987 - D. Nargiso (Italy)
1988 - N. Pereira (Venezuela)
1989 - N. Kulti (Sweden)
1990 - L. Paes (India)
1991 - T. Enquist (Sweden)
1992 - D. Skoch (Czechoslovakia)
1993 - R. Sabau (Romania)
1994 - S. Humphries (U.S.A.)
1995 - O. Mutis (France)

BOYS' DOUBLES

1982 - P. Cash and J. Frawley
1983 - M. Kratzmann and S. Youl
1984 - R. Brown and R. Weiss
1985 - A. Moreno and J. Yzaga
1986 - T. Carbonell and P. Korda

1987 - J. Stoltenberg and T. Woodbridge
1988 - J. Stoltenberg and T. Woodbridge
1989 - J. Palmer and J. Stark
1990 - S. Lareau and S. Leblanc
1991 - K. Alami and G. Rusedski

1992 - S. Baldas and S. Draper
1993 - S. Downs and J. Greenhalgh
1994 - B. Ellwood and M. Philippoussis
1995 - M. Lee and J.M. Trotman

GIRLS' SINGLES

1948 - Miss O. Miskova (Czechoslovakia)
1949 - Miss C. Mercelis (Belgium)
1950 - Miss L. Cornell (G.B.)
1951 - Miss L. Cornell (G.B.)
1952 - Miss ten Bosch (Netherlands)
1953 - Miss D. Kilian (S.A.)
1954 - Miss V. A. Pitt (G.B.)
1955 - Miss S. M. Armstrong (G.B.)
1956 - Miss A. S. Haydon (G.B.)
1957 - Miss M. Arnold (U.S.A.)
1958 - Miss S. M. Moore (U.S.A.)
1959 - Miss J. Cross (S.A.)

1960 - Miss K. Hantze (U.S.A.)
1961 - Miss G. Baksheeva (U.S.S.R.)
1962 - Miss G. Baksheeva (U.S.S.R.)
1963 - Miss D. M. Salfati (France)
1964 - Miss P. Bartkowicz (U.S.A.)
1965 - Miss O. Morozova (U.S.S.R.)
1966 - Miss B. Lindstrom (Finland)
1967 - Miss J. Salome (Netherlands)
1968 - Miss K. Pigeon (U.S.A.)
1969 - Miss K. Sawamatsu (Japan)
1970 - Miss S. Walsh (U.S.A.)
1971 - Miss M. Kroschina (U.S.S.R.)

1972 - Miss I. Kloss (S.A.)
1973 - Miss A. Kiyomura (U.S.A.)
1974 - Miss M. Jausovec (Yugoslavia)
1975 - Miss N. Y. Chmyreva (U.S.S.R.)
1976 - Miss N. Y. Chmyreva (U.S.S.R.)
1977 - Miss L. Antonoplis (U.S.A.)
1978 - Miss T. Austin (U.S.A.)
1979 - Miss M. L. Piatek (U.S.A.)
1980 - Miss D. Freeman (Australia)
1981 - Miss Z. Garrison (U.S.A.)
1982 - Miss C. Tanvier (France)
1983 - Miss P. Paradis (France)

1984 - Miss A. N. Croft (G.B.)
1985 - Miss A. Holikova (Czechoslovakia)
1986 - Miss N. Zvereva (U.S.S.R.)
1987 - Miss N. Zvereva (U.S.S.R.)
1988 - Miss B. Schultz (Netherlands)
1989 - Miss A. Strnadova (Czechoslavakia)
1990 - Miss A. Strnadova (Czechoslavakia)
1991 - Miss B. Rittner (Germany)
1992 - Miss C. Rubin (U.S.A.)
1993 - Miss N. Feber (Belgium)
1994 - Miss M. Hingis (Switzerland)
1995 - Miss A. Olsza (Poland)

GIRLS' DOUBLES

1982 - Miss B. Herr and Miss P. Barg
1983 - Miss P. Fendick and Miss P. Hy
1984 - Miss C. Kuhlman and Miss S. Rehe
1985 - Miss L. Field and Miss J. Thompson
1986 - Miss M. Jaggard and Miss L. O'Neill

1987 - Miss N. Medvedeva and Miss N. Zvereva
1988 - Miss J. A. Faull and Miss R. McQuillan
1989 - Miss J. Capriati and Miss M. McGrath
1990 - Miss K. Habsudova and Miss A. Strnadova
1991 - Miss C. Barclay and Miss L. Zaltz

1992 - Miss M. Avotins and Miss L. McShea
1993 - Miss L. Courtois and Miss N. Feber
1994 - Miss E. De Villiers and Miss E. E. Jelfs
1995 - Miss C. Black and Miss A. Olsza